Harmony in Hearts: Positive Psychology Practices for Lasting Marriages

By

Don J. Mathis

Presentation

Welcome to "Harmony in Hearts: Positive Psychology Practices for Lasting Marriages." amid life's intricacies, challenges, and delights, the excursion of marriage remains a demonstration of the getting through force of adoration, association, and responsibility. In these pages, we set out on an excursion of investigation, revelation, and change — an excursion directed by the standards of positive brain research and energised by the conviction that each marriage can prosper and flourish. In the embroidery of human connections, marriage consumes a sacrosanct space — an association of hearts, psyches, and spirits bound together by affection, shared values, and a common vision for what's in store. However, similar to any travel worth leaving upon, the way of marriage isn't without its turns, turns, and incidental diversions. It is an excursion set apart by snapshots of bliss and festivity, as well as snapshots of challenge and development — an excursion that requires boldness, versatility, and a profound obligation to the prosperity of the two accomplices.

"Harmony in Hearts" is something beyond a book — it is an aide, a sidekick, and a wellspring of motivation for couples trying to develop further association, shared understanding, and enduring bliss in their relationships. Drawing upon the standards of positive brain research, we investigate the study of satisfaction, flexibility, and flourishing connections, offering viable devices, activities, and experiences to assist couples with making an underpinning of concordance, love, and euphoria in their coexistence.

As we venture together through the pages of "Harmony in Hearts," we will investigate the accompanying key subjects:

1. The Study of Happiness: We dive into the standards of positive brain research, investigating the elements that add to joy, satisfaction, and prosperity in marriage. From appreciation and care to flexibility and reason, we uncover the key to developing a prospering marriage established in energy and love.

2. Building Flexibility and Conquering Challenges: We go up against the unavoidable difficulties and snags that emerge in marriage, offering techniques for building

versatility, exploring clashes, and defeating affliction with elegance and empathy. Through open correspondence, sympathy, and a common obligation to development, couples can change difficulties into potential open doors for more profound association and shared understanding.

3. Cultivating Association and Intimacy: We investigate the significance of sustaining close-to-home closeness, cultivating significant association, and reigniting the flash of enthusiasm and sentiment in marriage. From main avenues for affection and correspondence procedures to closeness-building activities and ceremonies of association, we offer pragmatic devices and experiences to assist couples with developing their bond and making snapshots of bliss and association.

4. Embracing Development and Transformation: We commend the excursion of development, investigation, and self-disclosure that unfurls inside the setting of marriage. From embracing change and vulnerability to encouraging individual and aggregate development, we welcome couples to leave on an excursion of change — an excursion that praises the remarkable gifts, qualities, and goals of each accomplice.

In the pages that follow, may you track down motivation, direction, and support to develop congruity, love, and satisfaction in your marriage. May "Harmony in Hearts" act as an encouraging sign, a wellspring of shrewdness, and an update that the excursion of marriage is a consecrated dance — a steadily developing festival of adoration, association, and shared dreams.

With open hearts and psyches, let us set out on this excursion together, embracing the magnificence, intricacy, and endless conceivable outcomes that look for us on the way to enduring concordance in our souls and our relationships.

Warm respects,

[Don J. Mathis]

Chapter 1:

Introduction to Positive Psychology in Marriage

In the hallowed association of marriage, the standards of positive brain research offer a signal of light — a directing structure that enlightens the way to more profound association, enduring bliss, and significant satisfaction. In Part 1, we leave on an excursion of investigation and revelation, establishing the groundwork for a marriage established in energy, flexibility, and common flourishing.

1. Understanding Positive Psychology: We start by investigating the quintessence of positive brain research — a study of prosperity, versatility, and thriving that spotlights the qualities, ideals, and potential for development inside people and connections. Positive brain research welcomes us to move our concentration from only resolving issues and shortages to sustaining qualities, encouraging flexibility, and developing joy and satisfaction in marriage.

2. The Influence of Positivity: We dig into the groundbreaking influence of energy in marriage, investigating how developing positive feelings, perspectives, and ways of behaving can improve the nature of our connections and upgrade our general prosperity. From appreciation and hopefulness to thoughtful gestures and care, we uncover the heap manners by which energy can extend our association with our accomplices and encourage a feeling of bliss, appreciation, and happiness in our coexistence.

3. Thriving Relationships: We investigate the signs of flourishing connections — those described by trust, closeness, and common help. Drawing upon the standards of positive brain science, we uncover the key fixings that add to the flourishing of relationships, including open correspondence, sympathy, shared objectives, and a profound feeling of association and having a place.

4. Resilience and Growth: We face the unavoidable difficulties and mishaps that emerge in marriage, remembering them not as dangers to the relationship but rather as any open doors for development, learning, and versatility. From the perspective of positive brain science, we investigate systems for building flexibility, exploring misfortune, and arising more grounded and joined as accomplices.

5. Cultivating Meaning and Purpose: We dig into the significance of developing importance and reason in marriage — of making a common vision, seeking after shared objectives, and finding satisfaction in serving an option that could be more significant than ourselves. From shared ceremonies and customs to demonstrations of administration and philanthropy, we find how imbuing our relationships with significance and reason can develop our association and support us through life's difficulties.

In Section 1, we lay the foundation for a marriage established in the standards of positive brain science — a marriage described by adoration, happiness, strength, and shared flourishing. As we set out on this excursion together, may we embrace the groundbreaking force of energy, flexibility, and common perspective, realising that through our obligation to development and association, we can make a marriage that isn't just persevering but genuinely phenomenal.

With open hearts and brains, let us set out on this excursion of investigation and disclosure, realising that the way forward is loaded up with limitless opportunities for affection, development, and satisfaction.

Warm respects,

[Don J. Mathis]

Defining positive psychology and its application in the context of marriage

Positive brain science is a part of brain science that spotlights understanding and encouraging human qualities, ethics, and prosperity, instead of exclusively tending to shortages and pathology. It investigates the elements that add to a satisfying and significant life, stressing positive feelings, character qualities, versatility, and self-improvement. With regards to marriage, positive brain research offers an extraordinary system for developing further association, versatility, and bliss in connections.

1. Emphasising Qualities and Virtues: Positive brain research in marriage moves the concentration from fixing issues to sustaining qualities and excellencies inside the relationship. It urges couples to distinguish and use their individual and aggregate qualities, like benevolence, sympathy, appreciation, and pardoning, to encourage a flourishing organisation based on common regard and understanding.

2. Cultivating Positive Emotions: Positive brain research features the significance of developing positive feelings, like love, euphoria, appreciation, and hopefulness, inside the conjugal relationship. By deliberately sustaining positive feelings, couples make a strong and inspiring environment that reinforces their security and upgrades their general prosperity.

3. Fostering Resilience: Versatility is a focal principle of positive brain science, stressing the capacity to quickly return from misfortune and develop through life's difficulties. In marriage, developing flexibility includes creating successful survival techniques, encouraging a feeling of positive thinking and trust, and keeping a profound association with one's accomplice during troublesome times. By building strength together, couples can weather conditions like storms and arise more grounded and joined than previously.

4. Promoting Meaning and Purpose: Positive brain research urges couples to track down significance and reason in their relationship by adjusting their qualities, objectives, and yearnings. By taking part in shared exercises, chasing after normal interests, and supporting each other's self-improvement and satisfaction, couples have a feeling of direction that enhances their lives and fortifies their bond.

5. Enhancing Correspondence and Connection: Compelling correspondence and close-to-home association are fundamental parts of a flourishing marriage. Positive brain science accentuates the significance of open, genuine correspondence, undivided attention, and sympathy in encouraging profound close-to-home closeness and understanding between accomplices. By developing positive correspondence propensities and communicating appreciation and warmth routinely, couples reinforce their close-to-home association and construct a strong starting point for an enduring relationship.

In synopsis, positive brain science offers an all-encompassing and enabling way to deal with marriage, zeroing in on the qualities, temperances, and positive feelings that add to a satisfying and significant organisation. By embracing the standards of positive brain research in their relationship, couples can develop flexibility, extend their association, and make a marriage that is portrayed by adoration, happiness, and common flourishing.

Exploring the Importance of Fostering Positivity, Resilience, and Emotional Well-being in Marital Relationships

In the embroidery of marriage, encouraging energy, strength, and profound prosperity fill in as the dynamic strings that wind around together the texture of a solid, satisfying organisation. As couples explore the delights and difficulties of coexistence, developing these characteristics becomes fundamental for building a groundwork of affection, trust, and shared help. We should investigate why encouraging energy, strength, and close-to-home prosperity is vital in conjugal connections:

1. Nurturing Positivity: Inspiration mixes marriage with warmth, euphoria, and appreciation, making an environment of appreciation and association between accomplices. At the point when couples develop an uplifting perspective, they are bound to zero in on one another's assets, celebrate shared snapshots of delight, and move toward difficulties with idealism and strength. Inspiration goes about as an impetus for more profound close-to-home closeness and reinforces the connection between accomplices, encouraging a feeling of appreciation and love that supports the relationship through both radiant days and blustery evenings.

2. Building Resilience: Flexibility is the foundation of a flourishing marriage, enabling couples to explore difficulty, defeat mishaps, and arise more grounded and joined than previously. Notwithstanding life's inescapable difficulties, strong couples draw upon their inward strength, shared values, and common help to weather conditions and storms and develop through difficulty together. By embracing difficulties as any open doors for development and learning, couples develop strength that extends their association and invigorates their obligation to one another.

3. Prioritising Close-to-Home Well-being: Profound prosperity shapes the bedrock of a solid, flourishing marriage, supporting the psychological, close-to-home, and otherworldly strength of the two accomplices. Couples who focus on close-to-home prosperity focus on open correspondence, undivided attention, and compassion, establishing a protected and strong climate where the two accomplices feel seen, heard, and esteemed. By going to one another's feelings and encouraging a culture of common regard and understanding, couples develop close-to-home flexibility and brace their bond against the burdens and kinds of day-to-day existence.

4. Promoting Development and Development: Encouraging energy, versatility, and close-to-home prosperity in marriage advance individual and aggregate development and improvement. As couples support each other's very own desires, dreams, and objectives, they establish a powerful climate where each accomplice feels engaged to seek after their interests and realise their true capacity. By embracing a development mentality and praising each other's accomplishments and achievements, couples cultivate a culture of consolation, motivation, and shared help that moves them forward on their excursion together.

5. Creating a Culture of Appreciation: Energy, flexibility, and profound prosperity in marriage are supported through a culture of appreciation and appreciation. Couples who routinely express appreciation, warmth, and profound respect for one another develop a feeling of association and closeness that reinforces their bond and supports their relationship over the long haul. By recognizing each other's commitments, insisting on each other's assets, and offering affection and thanks uninhibitedly, couples make a supply of generosity and love that enhances their marriage and sustains their spirits.

Generally, encouraging energy, strength, and profound prosperity in conjugal connections lays the preparation for an affection that perseveres — an adoration that maintains, supports, and elevates the two accomplices through life's horde experiences and difficulties. As couples embrace these characteristics, they make a haven of affection, trust, and shared understanding — an asylum where hearts find comfort, spirits track down reestablishment, and love tracks down its most genuine articulation.

Chapter 2:

The Foundations of Lasting Marriages

In the perplexing woven artwork of marriage, certain fundamental components act as support points whereupon persevering through adoration, trust, and closeness are fabricated. Part 2 digs into these central standards, enlightening the fundamental characteristics and practices that lay the preparation for enduring and satisfying relationships. As couples set out on the excursion of long-lasting organisation, understanding and exemplifying these fundamental components become fundamental for sustaining a relationship that goes the distance.

1. Trust and Transparency: At the core of every enduring marriage lies trust — a profound and relentless confidence in one another's genuineness, uprightness, and responsibility. Trust is supported through straightforwardness, open correspondence, and a common obligation to genuineness and credibility. Couples who focus on trust are free from any potentially harmful starting point for their relationship, permitting them to explore difficulties with certainty and common regard.

2. Communication and Connection: Powerful correspondence is the backbone of marriage, cultivating figuring out, compassion, and close-to-home closeness between accomplices. Section 2 investigates the significance of clear, legitimate correspondence, undivided attention, and approval of one another's viewpoints. Couples who focus on correspondence make a culture of transparency and weakness, developing their association and fortifying their bond.

3. Shared Values and Goals: Enduring relationships are grounded in shared values, objectives, and yearnings that join accomplices in a typical reason. By adjusting their vision for the future and embracing normal qualities, couples create a feeling of solidarity and reason that guides them through life's promising and less promising times. Section 2 urges couples to investigate their common qualities and dreams, encouraging a feeling of organisation and cooperation that enhances their relationship.

4. Resilience and Adaptability: The excursion of marriage is loaded up with startling exciting bends in the road, requesting versatility, and flexibility from the two accomplices. Part 2 investigates the significance of embracing change, exploring difficulties, and developing all together. Couples who develop flexibility in weather conditions storm with beauty and mettle, arising more grounded and more joined despite affliction.

5. Emotional Closeness and Affection: Profound closeness shapes the underpinning of profound and significant associations in marriage, cultivating a feeling of closeness, acknowledgment, and having a place between accomplices. Part 2 dives into the significance of communicating fondness, supporting profound securities, and focusing on quality time together. Couples who focus on close-to-home closeness make a haven of affection and backing, where the two accomplices feel loved and esteemed.

6. Commitment and Dedication: Enduring relationships are supported by a profound and withstanding obligation to one another's prosperity and joy. Section 2 investigates the significance of devotion, dedication, and persistence notwithstanding challenges. Couples who stay resolute in their responsibility endure the hardships of existence with flexibility and elegance, manufacturing a bond that develops further as time passes.

In synopsis, Part 2 lays the basis for enduring and satisfying relationships by investigating the fundamental components that support love, trust, and closeness over the long run. By embracing trust, correspondence, shared values, versatility, profound closeness, and responsibility, couples make a strong groundwork whereupon their relationship can prosper and flourish. As couples typify these essential standards, they prepare for a long period of affection, association, and shared satisfaction.

Examining the major standards of fruitful relationships, including correspondence, trust, regard, and closeness

Effective relationships are based upon a groundwork of trust, correspondence, regard, and closeness — key rules that structure the bedrock of persevering through affection and organisation. In the sacrosanct excursion of marriage, understanding and typifying these standards are fundamental for developing a relationship that flourishes through life's heavy delights and difficulties. We should investigate every one of these standards top to bottom:

1. Communication: Viable correspondence is the foundation of an effective marriage, encouraging grasping, sympathy, and association between accomplices. Couples who focus on open, legitimate correspondence establish a protected and steady climate where contemplations, sentiments, and concerns can be shared straightforwardly and without judgement. Correspondence includes undivided attention, putting oneself out there plainly and deferentially, and being open to one another's points of view. By developing a culture of correspondence, couples extend their bond, resolve clashes productively, and support a feeling of closeness and trust.

2. Trust: Trust is the establishment whereupon enduring relationships are constructed — a profound and faithful confidence in one another's genuineness, unwavering quality, and responsibility. Trust is sustained through reliable activities, straightforwardness, and uprightness in all parts of the relationship. Couples who trust each other certainly have a feeling of safety and strength that permits their adoration to prosper. Trust empowers accomplices to be defenceless, to rest on one another in hardship, and to weather conditions and difficulties with certainty and common help.

3. Respect: Regard frames the premise of common appreciation, profound respect, and thought in marriage. Couples who regard each other's considerations, sentiments, and limits make an organisation portrayed by pride and honour. Regard includes esteeming each other's points of view, respecting contrasts, and treating each other with generosity and sympathy. By encouraging a climate of regard, couples develop a feeling of balance and shared respect that reinforces their bond and improves their close-to-home association.

4. Intimacy: Profound and actual closeness are fundamental parts of a satisfying marriage, encouraging a profound feeling of association, having a place, and warmth between accomplices. Profound closeness includes sharing weaknesses, dreams, and desires, making a feeling of closeness and understanding that ties hearts together. Actual closeness incorporates tokens of warmth, closeness, and sexual articulation that support the body and soul. Couples who focus on closeness develop a feeling of warmth, enthusiasm, and association that improves their relationship and supports their affection over the long haul.

By embracing the central standards of correspondence, trust, regard, and closeness, couples make a strong groundwork whereupon their marriage can prosper and flourish. These standards act as directing lights, enlightening the way to more profound association, common comprehension, and enduring satisfaction in marriage. As couples epitomise these standards in their regular routines, they make a haven of affection, trust, and backing — a haven where hearts find comfort, spirits track down reestablishment, and love tracks down its most genuine articulation.

Introducing the role of positive psychology in strengthening these foundational aspects

Positive brain science offers an extraordinary focal point through which couples can extend how they might interpret essential viewpoints like correspondence, trust, regard, and closeness in marriage. By coordinating the standards of positive brain research into their relationship, couples can develop a more profound feeling of association, flexibility, and satisfaction. We should investigate how positive brain science fortifies these central angles:

1. Communication: Positive brain research underscores the significance of positive correspondence designs that cultivate compassion, understanding, and association between accomplices. Couples can figure out how to zero in on qualities, offer thanks, and take part in undivided attention, establishing a strong climate where correspondence streams openly and truly. Positive correspondence strategies, like utilising "I" proclamations, communicating appreciation, and looking for a shared belief, empower couples to explore clashes helpfully and develop their close-to-home security.

2. Trust: Positive brain research urges couples to develop trust through thoughtful gestures, unwavering quality, and honesty. By zeroing in on qualities and expanding on past triumphs, couples can fortify their confidence in one another's generosity and responsibility. Through trust-building works, couples can investigate their weaknesses, express sympathy, and foster a more profound comprehension of one another's requirements and wants. Positive brain research cultivates a feeling of good faith and trust, permitting couples to move toward difficulties with versatility and common help.

3. Respect: Positive brain research underlines the significance of common regard and appreciation in marriage. Couples can develop regard by recognizing each other's assets, insisting on their qualities, and respecting their disparities. Through care rehearses, couples can turn out to be more receptive to one another's necessities and feelings, cultivating a culture of empathy and acknowledgment. Positive brain research urges couples to commend variety and embrace each other's novel points of view, making a feeling of solidarity and common respect that reinforces their bond.

4. Intimacy: Positive brain science perceives the meaning of profound and actual closeness in advancing conjugal fulfilment and prosperity. Couples can upgrade closeness by focusing on snapshots of association, communicating friendship, and participating in shared exercises that encourage a feeling of closeness and having a place. Through sure ceremonies of association, couples can set out open doors for delight, fun-loving nature, and sentiment, extending their profound bond and reigniting the flash of enthusiasm in their relationship.

By coordinating the standards of positive brain science into their marriage, couples can change difficulties into open doors for development, extend their association, and develop a relationship that is portrayed by adoration, flexibility, and common flourishing. Positive brain research offers couples a guide for making a marriage that isn't just persevering but additionally profoundly satisfying — a marriage where correspondence streams uninhibitedly, trust proliferates, regard twists, and closeness blooms. As couples set out on this excursion of investigation and revelation, may they track down motivation, strength, and satisfaction in the groundbreaking force of positive brain research.

Chapter 3:

Cultivating Gratitude and Appreciation

In the nursery of marriage, appreciation and appreciation are the sustaining soil that supports love, trust, and association between accomplices. Section 3 investigates the significant effect of developing appreciation and appreciation in fortifying the obligations of marriage and encouraging a more profound feeling of closeness and satisfaction.

1. Understanding Appreciation: Appreciation is the act of recognizing and valuing the endowments, kindnesses, and delights present in our lives. With regards to marriage, appreciation includes perceiving and communicating appreciation for the characteristics, activities, and commitments of our accomplices. By developing a mentality of appreciation, couples hold nothing back from the overflow of affection, backing, and excellence that encompasses them, extending their appreciation for one another and their relationship.

2. The Force of Appreciation: Appreciation is the language of adoration — a useful asset for supporting association, approval, and confirmation in marriage. Section 3 investigates the groundbreaking effect of communicating authentic appreciation for our accomplices' endeavours, penances, and characteristics. At the point when accomplices feel seen, esteemed, and appreciated, they are bound to feel valued and upheld in their relationship, encouraging a feeling of shared regard and profound respect that reinforces their bond.

3. Practising Appreciation Customs: Part 3 presents useful systems and ceremonies for integrating appreciation and appreciation into day-to-day existence. From appreciation journaling and everyday reflections to communicating verbal certifications and thoughtful gestures, couples can make significant ceremonies that develop a culture of appreciation and appreciation in their marriage. By making appreciation a standard piece of their cooperation, couples develop their close-to-home association and make a repository of generosity and warmth that supports their relationship through both happy minutes and difficulties.

4. Navigating Difficulties with Appreciation: Appreciation fills in as a strong cure to pessimism, hatred, and struggle in marriage. Section 3 investigates how rehearsing appreciation can assist couples with exploring difficulties with strength, sympathy, and elegance. By reexamining tough spots from a perspective of appreciation, couples can track down silver linings, gain from difficulty, and develop nearer as accomplices. Appreciation encourages a feeling of point of view and strength that enables couples to confront difficulties with positive thinking and common help.

5. Celebrating Shared Snapshots of Bliss: Appreciation welcomes couples to celebrate and relish the common snapshots of satisfaction, chuckling, and association that improve their relationship. From basic joys to achievement accomplishments, couples can offer thanks for the gifts and encounters that unite them. By relishing these experiences of association and bliss, couples develop their appreciation for one another and make enduring recollections that reinforce the underpinning of their marriage.

In rundown, Section 3 urges couples to develop appreciation and appreciation as primary practices in their marriage. By embracing the force of appreciation, couples make a culture of adoration, benevolence, and association that feeds their relationship and supports their bond through life's high points and low points. As couples set out on the excursion of developing appreciation and appreciation, may they find the groundbreaking force of affection communicated through words, motions, and snapshots of shared satisfaction.

Exploring the transformative power of gratitude and appreciation in marriage

Appreciation and appreciation are not just feelings; they are extraordinary powers that can develop love, reinforce bonds, and raise the nature of conjugal connections. In the embroidery of marriage, the act of appreciation and appreciation fills in as a string that winds through each cooperation, implanting the relationship with warmth, association, and flexibility.

1. Cultivating Close to Home Connection: Appreciation and appreciation act as scaffolds that interface accomplices on a profound level. At the point when couples offer thanks for one another's presence, endeavours, and characteristics, they create a feeling of close-to-home closeness and approval that reinforces their bond. Feeling seen, esteemed, and valued by one's accomplice cultivates a profound feeling of having a place and security, sustaining a groundwork of trust and shared help in the relationship.

2. Fostering Positivity: Appreciation and appreciation go about as counteractants to pessimism and hatred, making a positive environment where love and graciousness can prosper. At the point when couples centre around the endowments and delights in their relationship, they shift their viewpoint based on the thing that is missing to what is plentiful. This change in mentality develops a feeling of hopefulness, flexibility, and happiness that implants each part of the marriage with warmth and imperativeness.

3. Enhancing Communication: Appreciation and appreciation act as strong types of correspondence, conveying affection, regard, and profound respect without the requirement for words. At the point when accomplices express appreciation for one another's endeavours, they approve and confirm the worth of those commitments, cultivating a culture of shared regard and consolation. By straightforwardly recognizing and offering thanks for one another's assets and characteristics, couples develop their profound association and establish a strong climate where the two accomplices feel esteemed and treasured.

4. Strengthening Resilience: Appreciation and appreciation outfit couples with the versatility expected to explore life's inescapable difficulties and misfortunes. At the point when accomplices approach challenges with appreciation, they shift their concentration from the issue to the arrangement, drawing strength from the help and love they share. By recognizing and valuing each other's endeavours to conquer snags, couples encourage a feeling of collaboration and shared strengthening that empowers them to weather conditions and storms with effortlessness and boldness.

5. Nurturing Sentiment and Intimacy: Appreciation and appreciation imbue sentiment and closeness with profundity and importance, making snapshots of association and closeness that develop the connection between accomplices. At the point when couples offer thanks for the little tokens of adoration and graciousness that improve their lives, they make an expanding influence of love and delicacy that supports the energy and sentiment in their relationship. By encouraging a culture of appreciation, couples make a haven of affection and warmth where closeness flourishes and hearts stay open to one another's touch.

Generally, the extraordinary force of appreciation and appreciation lies in their capacity to mix each snapshot of marriage with affection, consideration, and association. As couples embrace the act of appreciation and appreciation, they set out on an excursion of revelation — one that prompts further getting it, more prominent versatility, and persevering through adoration. Through the basic demonstration of saying "much obliged" and communicating appreciation for the endowment of one another, couples open the genuine embodiment of conjugal joy — an excursion of adoration, development, and shared delight that rises above the progression of time.

Providing practical exercises and techniques for cultivating gratitude and expressing appreciation within the marital relationship

Developing an appreciation and communicating appreciation inside a conjugal relationship is essential for encouraging areas of strength for getting through security. Here are a few reasonable activities and methods to assist with accomplishing this:

1. Gratitude Journaling: Urge each accomplice to keep an appreciation diary where they record three things they value about their mate consistently. This training helps centre around the positive parts of the relationship.

2. Daily Appreciation Rituals: Put away a couple of moments every day to communicate appreciation to one another. It may very well be during breakfast or before hitting the sack. Alternate offering thanks for explicit things your accomplice has done or characteristics you respect.

3. Surprise Badge of Appreciation: Leave little notes of appreciation in startling spots for your accomplice to find — a sincere message on the washroom reflect or a sweet note got into their wallet. These little signals can go quite far in causing your accomplice to feel esteemed.

4. Actively Listen: Practise undivided attention when your accomplice puts themselves out there. Focus on them without interfering, and answer with compassion and understanding. Feeling appreciated and recognized cultivates a feeling of appreciation.

5. Celebrate Achievements: Praise each other's achievements, regardless of how little. Perceive and recognize the endeavours your accomplice places into individual or expert objectives. Gathering together to celebrate fortifies your security and builds up shared help.

6. Gratitude Walks: Go for strolls together and verbally offer thanks for the things around you and one another's presence. Getting a charge out of nature while communicating appreciation can extend your association.

7. Weekly Appreciation Rituals: Commit a particular time every week to plunk down together and share the things you are thankful for in your relationship. Consider the ups and downs of the week and offer thanks for the difficulties you've defeated together.

8. Random Demonstrations of Kindness: Shock your collaboration with thoughtful gestures that show appreciation — make their #1 dinner, assume control over an errand they dislike, or plan an unconstrained night out. These acts of kindness build up your affection and appreciation for one another.

9. Express Love Languages: Learn and see each other's ways to express affection. Tailor your looks of appreciation and appreciation to line up with your accomplice's inclinations, whether it's through encouraging statements, demonstrations of administration, quality time, actual touch, or getting gifts.

10. Reflect on Shared Memories: Find an opportunity to think back about blissful recollections and achievements you've shared as a couple. Pondering the excursion you've been on together can bring out sensations of appreciation and fortify your profound association.

By integrating these activities and strategies into your day-to-day routines, you can support a culture of appreciation and appreciation inside your conjugal relationship, cultivating adoration, association, and common regard.

Chapter 4:

Embracing Positive Thinking and Trust

In the excursion of life and connections, embracing good faith and trust fills in as a directing light through difficulties and vulnerabilities. This section digs into the significance of keeping an uplifting perspective and encouraging expectation, even notwithstanding difficulty.

1. Understanding Good Faith: Idealism isn't only about living in a fantasy land; a mentality empowers people and couples to consider difficulties to open doors for development. It includes zeroing in on the potential outcomes as opposed to harping on misfortunes. This segment investigates the force of positive reasoning and its effect on mental prosperity.

2. Cultivating Strength: Flexibility is the capacity to return from misfortunes and endure notwithstanding difficulty. By developing flexibility, couples can weather conditions and storms together and arise more grounded. Techniques for building versatility, for example, creating critical thinking abilities and keeping an encouraging group of people, are examined to engage couples in exploring life's highs and lows.

3. Nurturing Expectation: Trust fills the soul and touches off the conviction that better days lie ahead. This part underscores the significance of supporting expectations inside oneself and the relationship. By putting forth reasonable objectives, envisioning achievement, and finding significance in troublesome conditions, couples can develop a feeling of trust that supports them through testing times.

4. Positive Correspondence Examples: Successful correspondence is fundamental for encouraging confidence and trust in the relationship. Couples are urged to rehearse positive correspondence designs, for example, offering thanks, offering uplifting statements, and zeroing in on arrangements as opposed to harping on issues. By sustaining a steady and elevating correspondence style, couples can build up positive thinking and trust in their relationship.

5. Creating a Dream for What's to Come: Shared dreams and desires provide couples with a feeling of motivation and heading. This segment investigates the most common way of making a dream for the future together, defining objectives that line up with their qualities and goals. By imagining a splendid future loaded with conceivable outcomes, couples can remain persuaded and confident amid life's vulnerabilities.

6. Mindfulness and Presence: Care rehearses assist couples with remaining grounded right now, cultivating a feeling of appreciation and appreciation for the present time and place. By developing care together, couples can fortify their bond and track down comfort in one another's presence, paying little heed to outer conditions.

7. Celebrating Advancement: Celebrating little triumphs and achievements en route builds up idealism and trust inside the relationship. This part stresses the significance of recognizing progress and development, regardless of how steady. By praising each other's accomplishments, couples reaffirm their faith in one another's true capacity and flexibility.

Fundamentally, embracing good faith and trust isn't tied in with denying the presence of difficulties but rather turning around them with boldness, strength, and confidence in the force of energy. By developing these characteristics inside themselves and their relationship, couples can explore life's excursion with effortlessness, good faith, and a resolute feeling of trust.

Discussing the significance of optimism and hope in navigating challenges and setbacks

Positive thinking and trust are primary components in the human experience, offering fundamental help in exploring life's hardships. In this aide, we dig into the significant meaning of confidence and trust even with difficulties and misfortunes, investigating their jobs, benefits, and commonsense applications.

Grasping Idealism and Trust

- **Optimism:** Idealism is the propensity to keep an uplifting perspective, even notwithstanding difficulty. It includes accepting that ideal results are conceivable and that hardships are transitory and conquerable.

- **Hope:** Trust is the assumption and craving for positive results, joined by the conviction that one can impact those results. It envelops both hopefulness and office, rousing people to persist regardless of obstructions.

The Job of Good Faith and Trust

1. Resilience: Good faith and trust develop versatility, empowering people to quickly return from mishaps with reestablished assurance and life.

2. Motivation: Idealism and trust fuel inspiration, moving people to seek after their objectives with excitement and tirelessness, even in testing conditions.

3. Emotional Well-being: Confidence and trust advance close-to-home prosperity by encouraging positive feelings, buffering against pressure, and giving a feeling of motivation and significance.

4. Problem-Solving: Confidence and trust energise productive critical thinking, as people approach difficulties with an arrangements-situated outlook and faith in their ability to defeat hindrances.

5. Relationships: Good faith and trust add to sound connections, encouraging trust, backing, and versatility in relational associations.

Advantages of Developing Good faith and Trust

1. Improved Adapting Skills: Hopeful people will generally adapt all the more actually to stress and difficulty, utilising versatile systems like looking for social help, reevaluating difficulties, and keeping up with viewpoints.

2. Enhanced Actual Health: Exploration recommends that confidence is related to better actual well-being results, including lower paces of cardiovascular illness, worked on safe capability, and expanded life span.

3. Greater Achievement: Hopeful people are bound to lay out aggressive objectives, endure despite difficulties, and at last make progress in different spaces of life, including scholastics, profession, and individual connections.

4. Enhanced Well-being: Developing good faith and trust adds to more prominent generally speaking prosperity, including more elevated levels of life fulfilment, joy, and emotional prosperity.

Viable Procedures for Developing Good faith and Trust

1. Cultivate Gratitude: Rehearsing appreciation encourages an uplifting perspective by zeroing in consideration on the endowments and open doors present in one's life.

2. Challenge Negative Thinking: Perceive and challenge negative idea designs, supplanting them with additional decent and hopeful points of view.

3. Set Reasonable Goals: Set clear, reachable objectives that motivate trust and give an internal compass and inspiration.

4. Practice Self-Compassion: Treat yourself with thoughtfulness and understanding, perceiving that mishaps are a characteristic piece of the human experience.

5. Seek Social Support: Encircle yourself with steady companions, relatives, and coaches who can give consolation, direction, and point of view during testing times.

All in all, good faith and trust are priceless resources in exploring life's difficulties and mishaps. By developing good faith, sustaining trust, and embracing a strong mentality, people can defy misfortune with boldness, assurance, and relentless confidence in the chance of a more promising time to come.

Strategies for Fostering a Positive Outlook and Maintaining Hopefulness Within the Marital Bond

An inspirational perspective and supported cheerfulness are fundamental elements for flourishing conjugal security. In this aide, we investigate useful techniques that couples can carry out to develop idealism, sustain trust, and reinforce their relationship through shared help and support.

1. Open Correspondence

- Straightforward Dialogue: Energise transparent correspondence, making a place of refuge where the two accomplices feel appreciated, comprehended, and regarded.

- Express Gratitude: Consistently offer appreciation and thanks for one another's commitments, signals, and characteristics, encouraging a feeling of shared appreciation and energy.

2. Developing Strength

- Recognize Challenges: Perceive that difficulties are a characteristic piece of any relationship and move toward them as any open doors for development and learning.

- Fabricate Adapting Skills: Foster successful ways of dealing with especially difficult times together, for example, critical thinking systems, stress-the-board methods, and solid compromise abilities.

3. Shared Objectives and Dreams

- Vision Building: Cooperatively imagine the future you want as a team, laying out shared objectives, desires, and dreams that motivate trust and solidarity.

- Observe Achievements: Recognize and praise achievements and accomplishments en route, supporting a feeling of progress and achievement.

4. Focus on Quality Time

- Quality Over Quantity: Spotlight on the nature of time spent together as opposed to the sheer amount, taking part in significant discussions, shared exercises, and encounters that fortify your bond.

- Plan Standard Date Nights: Devote time for normal date evenings or excursions to reconnect, loosen up, and appreciate each other's conversation without interruptions.

5. Steady Attitude

- Be Each Other's Cheerleader: Offer immovable help, support, and insistence to your accomplice, particularly during seasons of vulnerability or affliction.

- Observe Each Other's Strengths: Perceive and commend each other's assets, gifts, and accomplishments, encouraging a feeling of common regard and esteem.

6. Encourage Profound Closeness

- Embrace Vulnerability: Establish a safe and sustaining climate where the two accomplices feel open to communicating their feelings, fears, and weaknesses without judgement.

- Practice Empathy: Develop compassion and understanding towards your accomplice's viewpoints, feelings, and encounters, cultivating further close-to-home association and closeness.

7. Develop Energy

- Zero in on Solutions: Shift centre from issues to arrangements, taking on a proactive outlook that underscores cooperation, imagination, and versatility.

- Track down Euphoria in Regular Moments: Develop a propensity for care and appreciation, finding satisfaction and excellence in the straightforward delights of day-to-day existence together.

All in all, cultivating an uplifting perspective and keeping up with confidence inside the conjugal bond requires purposeful exertion, responsibility, and shared help. By focusing on open correspondence, developing flexibility, sharing objectives and dreams, focusing on quality time, embracing a steady mentality, encouraging close-to-home closeness, and developing energy, couples can sustain major areas of strength for a persevering relationship based on adoration, trust, and shared confidence for what's to come.

Chapter 5:

Nurturing Love and Compassion

In the excursion of self-awareness and human association, Section 5 digs into the significant meaning of sustaining affection and empathy. It highlights the groundbreaking influence of these ethics in enhancing individual lives and encouraging agreeable connections inside networks. Love, in its bunch structures, arises as a directing power fit for rising above boundaries and developing sympathy. It envelops confidence, empathy for other people, and an appreciation for the interconnectedness of mankind. Through contemplation and care, people set out on a way of self-revelation, perceiving their innate value and embracing weakness as a foundation of bona fide association.

Sympathy, the embodiment of compassion in real life, powers selflessness and generosity towards oneself as well as other people. It includes taking the stand concerning enduring with an open heart and expanding compassion without judgment. By developing a caring mentality, people develop strength, extend relational bonds, and add to aggregate recuperating and social union. The section investigates pragmatic methodologies for developing adoration and sympathy in day-to-day existence, underlining the significance of compassion, undivided attention, and thoughtful gestures. It features the groundbreaking capability of absolution and acknowledgment in delivering disdain and cultivating close-to-home freedom.

Moreover, the part highlights the job of the local area and aggregates help in supporting adoration and sympathy. Through significant associations and cooperative undertakings, people enhance their ability for sympathy and develop a common feeling of direction established in help and fortitude.

Generally, Part 5 fills in as a powerful sign of the intrinsic human limit concerning cherishing and empathy. It moves pursuers to develop these temperances as core values in exploring life's intricacies, cultivating further associations, and embracing the intrinsic magnificence of the human experience.

Exploring the concept of love as a foundational element in marriage

Investigating the idea of adoration as a fundamental component in marriage is a profoundly private and multifaceted excursion that includes understanding, supporting, and developing comprehension one might interpret love inside the setting of a serious organisation. Love fills in as the bedrock whereupon the whole design of marriage is constructed, affecting the way that couples convey, associate, and explore the difficulties and delights of coexistence. In this aide, we'll dive into different parts of affection in marriage, including its definitions, parts, articulations, and practices for developing a flourishing conjugal bond.

1. Grasping the Idea of Affection:

- Characterise Love: Love includes a range of feelings, ways of behaving, and perspectives portrayed by warmth, sympathy, trust, regard, and closeness. A multi-layered idea shifts in power and articulation among people and societies.

- Kinds of Love: Investigate various sorts of adoration, for example, heartfelt love, friendship love, familial love, and genuine love. Perceive that adoration in marriage frequently consolidates components of each sort, developing and extending over the long run.

2. Parts of Adoration in Marriage:

- Profound Intimacy: Close-to-home closeness includes sharing weaknesses, fears, dreams, and desires with your accomplice. It encourages a profound feeling of association and grasping, establishing the groundwork for trust and shared help.

- Actual Affection: Actual fondness incorporates signals like embraces, kisses, nestling, and sexual closeness. These outflows of affection assume a vital part in holding couples together and building up profound closeness.

- Commitment: Responsibility connotes the devotion to the relationship and the readiness to manage difficulties, honour guarantees, and focus on the prosperity of the association above individual longings or clashes.

 3. Developing Affection in Marriage:

- Compelling Communication: Open, genuine, and aware correspondence is fundamental for building and supporting adoration in marriage. Practise undivided attention, compassion, and approval to productively figure out your accomplice's point of view and offer your viewpoints and sentiments.

- Quality Time Together: Devote standard opportunity to support your relationship and make significant recollections together. Whether through shared side interests, date evenings, or basic snapshots of association, focus on quality chances to reinforce your bond.

- Communicating Appreciation and Gratitude: Communicating appreciation for your accomplice's characteristics, endeavours, and commitments cultivates a positive climate of affection and approval inside the marriage. Consistently recognize and thank your accomplice for their presence and backing in your life.

- Regarding Differences: Perceive and regard each other's uniqueness, viewpoints, and limits. Embrace the variety of encounters and sentiments inside the marriage, cultivating a climate of acknowledgment and shared regard.

- Struggle Resolution: Conflicts and clashes are unavoidable in any relationship. Move toward clashes with persistence, sympathy, and an eagerness to find helpful arrangements together. Centre around grasping the fundamental feelings and requirements driving the contention, instead of looking to win or appoint fault.

4. Advancing Affection in Marriage:

- Variation and Growth: Love in marriage is dynamic and advances over the long run. Embrace the excursion of development and change as people and as a couple, perceiving that difficulties and changes are open doors for learning and extending your association.

- Deep-rooted Learning: Persistently investigate and find out about your accomplice's advancing requirements, wants, and goals. Develop interest and a feeling of experience in finding new features of your relationship and one another.

- Reviving Romance: Keep the fire of sentiment alive by taking part in unconstrained tokens of love, shock dates, or heartfelt escapes. Track down imaginative ways of reigniting the enthusiasm and energy inside your marriage, supporting the flash that at first united you.

Investigating the idea of adoration as a fundamental component in marriage requires a pledge to understand, support, and develop the diverse elements of affection inside the organisation. By developing close-to-home closeness, rehearsing viable correspondence, communicating appreciation, regarding contrasts, and embracing development together, couples can make a strong and satisfying conjugal security established in affection, trust, and shared regard. At last, love in marriage is a deep-rooted excursion of disclosure, association, and shared encounters, enhancing the two accomplices' lives and cultivating a profound feeling of having a place and friendship.

Presenting merciful correspondence, compassion, and understanding as fundamental parts of conjugal love

Presenting caring correspondence, sympathy, and understanding as fundamental parts of conjugal love lays the preparation for cultivating a profound association, shared regard, and close-to-home closeness inside the relationship. These components act as support points that help compelling correspondence, compromise, and the development of compassion in exploring the intricacies of hitched life. In this aide, we'll investigate how couples can coordinate caring correspondence, compassion, and understanding into their union to reinforce their bond and advance an agreeable organisation.

1. Humane Correspondence:

- Definition: Humane correspondence includes offering viewpoints, sentiments, and requirements with compassion, thoughtfulness, and regard for one as well as one's accomplice.

- Dynamic Listening: Practise undivided attention by offering your accomplice your full consideration, keeping in touch, and giving verbal and nonverbal signals that show you are locked in and open to their words.

- Validation: Approve your accomplice's encounters, feelings, and viewpoints by recognizing their sentiments and showing sympathy and understanding.

- Use "I" Statements: Offer your viewpoints, sentiments, and requirements utilizing "I" articulations to take responsibility for feelings and try not to find fault or analysis on your accomplice.

- Keep away from Protectiveness and Criticism: Cease from becoming cautious or basic during discussions. All things considered, move toward conversations with transparency, interest, and an eagerness to figure out your accomplice's perspective.

- Look for Normal Ground: Search for areas of understanding and shared belief during conversations, zeroing in on shared objectives, values, and desires that can reinforce your association as a team.

2. Compassion:

- Definition: Compassion includes the capacity to comprehend and partake in your accomplice's feelings, encounters, and viewpoints, regardless of whether they vary from your own.

- Put Yourself in Their Shoes: Practise sympathy by envisioning yourself in your accomplice's situation and taking into account how they may be feeling or encountering what is happening.

- Approve Emotions: Approve your accomplice's feelings by recognizing their sentiments and exhibiting sympathy, regardless of whether you essentially concur with their viewpoint.

- Intelligent Listening: Reflect on how you might interpret your accomplice's feelings and encounters to show that you are effectively tuning in and looking to grasp their perspective.

- Show Support: Offer basic encouragement and consolation to your accomplice during troublesome times, exhibiting your obligation to be their partner and compatriot.

3. Understanding:

- Develop Curiosity: Approach discussions with a feeling of interest and a certified craving to figure out your accomplice's considerations, sentiments, and inspirations.

- Ask Unconditional Questions: Energise transparent correspondence by posing unassuming inquiries that welcome your accomplice to completely share their considerations and sentiments more.

- Regard Differences: Perceive and regard the distinctions in viewpoints, encounters, and correspondence styles among you and your accomplice.

- Explain Intentions: Explain your aims and look for an explanation from your accomplice to guarantee shared understanding and stay away from errors or misinterpretations.

4. Rehearsing Caring Correspondence, Sympathy, and Understanding:

- Put Away Committed Time: Put away devoted time for significant discussions where you can zero in on rehearsing empathetic correspondence, compassion, and understanding without interruptions.

- Practice Patience: Develop persistence and care during conversations, permitting space for both you and your accomplice to communicate your thoughts completely and without judgement.

- Look for Proficient Support: If correspondence challenges persevere or become overpowering, consider looking for the direction of a couples specialist or mentor who can give devices and methodologies to further developing correspondence and figuring out inside your marriage.

Presenting sympathetic correspondence, sympathy, and understanding as fundamental parts of conjugal love establishes a steady and sustaining climate where couples can straightforwardly communicate their thoughts, approve of each other's encounters, and develop compassion and understanding. By integrating these components into their everyday collaborations and correspondence propensities, couples can develop their close-to-home association, reinforce their bond, and explore the difficulties and delights of hitched existence with beauty and empathy. Eventually, rehearsing sympathetic correspondence, sympathy, and grasping cultivates shared regard, trust, and closeness, establishing the groundwork for a versatile and satisfying conjugal relationship.

Chapter 6:

Building Flexibility and Versatility

In the excursion of marriage, building versatility and flexibility is likened to strengthening the groundwork of a durable house that endures everyday hardships, enduring tempests, and adjusting to evolving scenes. This part digs into the significance of versatility and flexibility in marriage and gives bits of knowledge and procedures to couples to develop these fundamental characteristics inside their relationship.

Grasping Flexibility and Versatility:

- Resilience: Flexibility in marriage alludes to the capacity to quickly return from difficulties, misfortunes, and clashes with strength, boldness, and a feeling of positive thinking. It includes developing close-to-home strength, critical thinking abilities, and a positive outlook to defeat misfortune and develop further as a couple.

- Adaptability: Flexibility involves the ability to change, develop, and flourish notwithstanding change, advances, and unanticipated conditions. It includes embracing adaptability, receptiveness, and imagination in exploring life's exciting bends in the road together, whether they be professional changes, migration, monetary vacillations, or well-being emergencies.

Methodologies for Building Versatility and Flexibility:

1. I Open and Fair Communication:

- Cultivate a culture of transparent correspondence where the two accomplices have a real sense of security and are upheld in offering their viewpoints, sentiments, and concerns.

- Support weakness and straightforwardness, sharing the two victories and battles, and cooperatively conceptualising answers for difficulties.

2. Cultivating Close to home Intelligence:

- Foster the capacity to appreciate anyone on a deeper level by expanding mindfulness, perceiving and dealing with feelings successfully, and compassionately grasping your accomplice's sentiments and points of view.

- Practice care strategies, like profound breathing, contemplation, or journaling, to remain grounded and focused during seasons of pressure or struggle.

3. Building a Help Network:

- Develop areas of strength for an organisation of companions, relatives, tutors, and individual couples who can give support, direction, and viewpoint during troublesome times.

- Search for proficient help from advisors, advocates, or care groups to explore complex issues and foster survival methods for overseeing pressure and affliction.

4. Nurturing the Relationship:

- Focus on quality time together to support the profound bond and association inside the relationship. Plan customary date evenings, end-of-the-week excursions, or shared exercises that cultivate closeness and make affectionate recollections.

- Express appreciation, appreciation, and friendship for your accomplice consistently, commending their assets, achievements, and commitments to the relationship.

5. Embracing Change and Growth:

- Embrace change as a characteristic and inescapable piece of life, seeing difficulties and changes as any open doors for learning, development, and self-revelation.

- Move toward change with a feeling of interest, adaptability, and versatility, investigating additional opportunities and pathways altogether.

6. Creating Customs of Resilience:

- Lay out customs or schedules that advance flexibility and fortify the close-to-home association between accomplices. This could incorporate morning appreciation works, evening reflections, or week-after-week registrations to evaluate the condition of the relationship and address any worries or clashes.

Building strength and flexibility in marriage is a continuous excursion that requires responsibility, persistence, and shared help from the two accomplices. By developing open correspondence, the capacity to understand individuals on a profound level, areas of strength for an organisation, and a versatile outlook, couples can explore life's difficulties with effortlessness, determination, and a feeling of common perspective. Eventually, the capacity to return from mishaps, adjust to change, and develop further together structures the bedrock of a strong and flourishing conjugal relationship that perseveres through the preliminaries and wins of life's excursion.

Discussing the importance of resilience in overcoming adversity and managing stressors within marriage

Talking about the significance of flexibility in conquering difficulty and overseeing stressors inside a marriage is pivotal for couples to explore the unavoidable difficulties and difficulties that emerge through their excursion together. Flexibility fills in as a primary quality that engages couples to return from mishaps, develop further even with misfortune, and extend their bond through shared encounters. In this aid, we'll investigate the meaning of strength in marriage and give experiences and systems for developing flexibility as a team.

1. Figuring out Strength in Marriage:

- Meaning of Resilience: Versatility alludes to the capacity to adjust, return, and flourish even with affliction, stress, and life's inescapable difficulties.

- Importance in Marriage: Versatility is fundamental in marriage as it empowers couples to weather conditions storms together, conquers hindrances, and arises more grounded from troublesome encounters. It cultivates a feeling of solidarity, trust, and common help, fortifying the underpinning of the relationship.

2. Significance of Versatility in Marriage:

- Exploring Life Transitions: Marriage includes exploring different life advances, for example, vocation changes, being a parent, movement, monetary vacillations, and well-being emergencies. Strength assists couples explore these advances with effortlessness and versatility, limiting the effect of stressors on the relationship.

- Overseeing Struggle and Communication: Versatility engages couples to oversee clashes helpfully, convey successfully, and resolve contrasts with compassion and understanding. It empowers them to return quickly from conflicts and mishaps, encouraging a culture of pardoning, splitting the difference, and common regard.

- Supporting Close to Home Well-being: Strength adds to the profound prosperity of the two accomplices, giving a cushion against wretchedness, nervousness, and burnout. It energises close-to-home closeness, weakness, and trust, making a place of refuge for accomplices to put themselves out there genuinely and look for help when required.

3. Procedures for Developing Versatility in Marriage:

- Creating Profound Intelligence: Develop the capacity to understand people at their core by expanding mindfulness, perceiving and dealing with feelings successfully, and relating to your accomplice's sentiments and points of view. Practice care and taking care of oneself methods to remain grounded and focused during seasons of pressure.

- Building a Help Network: Develop major areas of strength for an organisation of companions, relatives, tutors, and individual couples who can give consolation, direction, and point of view during troublesome times. Look for proficient help from specialists or advisors to explore complex issues and foster survival methods.

- Encouraging Open Communication: Cultivate a culture of transparent correspondence where the two accomplices have a real sense of security and are upheld in offering their viewpoints, sentiments, and concerns. Practice undivided attention, compassion, and approval to figure out your accomplice's point of view and convey actuality.

- Supporting the Relationship: Focus on quality time together to sustain the profound bond and association inside the relationship. Participate in shared exercises, offer appreciation and thanks for one another, and praise achievements and achievements as a team.

- Embracing Development Mindset: Embrace a development outlook that perspectives difficulties and mishaps as any open doors for learning, development, and self-disclosure. Move toward challenges with interest, versatility, and an eagerness to investigate additional opportunities and arrangements altogether.

In conclusion, Examining the significance of versatility in conquering difficulty and overseeing stressors inside marriage lays the foundation for building major areas of strength for a, and flourishing organisation. By understanding the meaning of flexibility, couples can develop the abilities, perspectives, and ways of behaving that are important to explore life's difficulties with beauty, strength, and solidarity. At last, flexibility engages couples to conquer deterrents, develop their bond, and establish a steady and sustaining climate where the two accomplices can thrive and develop together, even notwithstanding misfortune.

Giving versatility-building methods and survival techniques for couples confronting troublesome times

Couples confronting testing times frequently experience pressure, strain, and vulnerability. Notwithstanding, by carrying out versatility-building procedures and ways of dealing with hardship or stress, they can explore these challenges and arise more grounded together. Here is a top-to-bottom manual for assisting couples with encouraging flexibility and adapting successfully:

1. Open Correspondence:

• Empower transparent correspondence between accomplices. Make a place of refuge where the two people feel appreciated, comprehended, and regarded.

• Practise undivided attention without judgement. Consider your accomplice's sentiments and approve their encounters.

• Plan standard registrations to talk about worries, fears, and expectations straightforwardly.

2. Construct Trust:

• Reinforce trust through straightforwardness and dependability. Be trustworthy and finish responsibilities.

• Abstain from accusing or condemning one another, particularly during upsetting times. All things considered centres around finding arrangements together.

• Recognize each other's assets and endeavours, building up a feeling of organisation.

3. Foster Ways of dealing with stress:

• Recognize individual and shared methods for dealing with hardship or stress. Energise solid methods for dealing with stress like care, profound breathing activities, and actual work.

• Investigate unwinding strategies like reflection, yoga, or moderate muscle unwinding to decrease pressure and advance profound prosperity.

• Encourage imagination and humour as a source for pressure alleviation. Take part in exercises that give pleasure and giggling to your relationship.

4. Oversee Struggle Helpfully:

• Learn helpful compromise strategies. Centre around finding compromises and arrangements instead of raising struggles.

• Practice persistence and compassion during conflicts. Attempt to serenely grasp your accomplice's viewpoint and offer your viewpoints and sentiments.

• Enjoy reprieves assuming feelings run high, yet focus on settling clashes consciously and beneficially.

5. Focus on Taking care of oneself:

• Urge each other to focus on taking care of their schedules. Underline the significance of rest, sustenance, and practice in keeping up with physical and profound well-being.

• Put down stopping points to safeguard individual existence. Permit each other the opportunity to seek after individual interests and leisure activities.

• Look for help from companions, relatives, or expert guides when required. Perceive that looking for help is an indication of solidarity, not a shortcoming.

6. Develop Strength:

• Cultivate a development outlook inside your relationship. Embrace difficulties as any open doors for learning and development.

• Centre around arrangements as opposed to harping on issues. Separate overpowering undertakings into reasonable advances and celebrate little triumphs en route.

• Consider previous encounters of conquering misfortune together. Draw strength from flexibility-building minutes to explore current difficulties.

7. Support Close to home Association:

• Focus on close-to-home closeness and association in your relationship. Participate in significant discussions, share desires, and express appreciation for one another.

• Practice compassion and approval to establish a strong climate where the two accomplices feel comprehended and esteemed.

• Set aside a few minutes for shared exercises and ceremonies that reinforce your bond and support your obligation to one another.

8. Look for Proficient Help:

• Think about looking for direction from couples advisors or relationship guides. Proficient help can give significant bits of knowledge, instruments, and procedures for exploring troublesome times.

• Go to couples advising meetings together to resolve hidden issues, further develop relational abilities, and fortify your relationship establishment.

9. Observe Progress:

• Recognize and celebrate progress, regardless of how little. Perceive the endeavours you and your accomplice are making to conquer difficulties and become together.

• Offer thanks for one another's versatility, backing, and obligation to the relationship. Commend achievements and accomplishments along your excursion.

10. Remain Focused on One another:

• Build up your obligation to one another during testing times. Help yourselves to remember the affection, trust, and shared objectives that join you as a team.

• Remain patient and versatile, it is brief to know that troublesome times. Together, you can weather conditions and arise more grounded, more associated, and stronger than previously.

By carrying out these versatility-building methods and survival techniques, couples can explore troublesome times with effortlessness, empathy, and strength. Keep in mind that confronting difficulties together can extend your bond and prepare for a stronger and satisfying relationship over the long haul.

Chapter 7:

Upgrading The capacity to appreciate anyone at their core

Understanding and dealing with feelings is an indispensable part of individual and expert development. The capacity to understand people at their core (EI) assumes an urgent part in exploring connections, simply deciding, and making progress in different circles of life. In this part, we dive into techniques and practices to upgrade the ability to understand people at their core.

1. Self-mindfulness: The foundation of the ability to appreciate anyone on a deeper level is mindfulness. Empowering people to investigate their feelings, distinguish sets off, and comprehend their effect on contemplations and ways of behaving cultivates more prominent close-to-home understanding. Procedures, for example, journaling, care, and self-reflection can support fostering a more profound comprehension of one's close-to-home scene.

2. Self-guideline: Viable self-guideline includes the capacity to oversee motivations, control feelings, and adjust to evolving conditions. Strategies like profound breathing, moderate muscle unwinding, and mental rebuilding engage people to manage their close-to-home reactions and go with productive decisions even in testing circumstances.

3. Empathy: Sympathy frames the groundwork of significant associations and successful correspondence. Empowering sympathy includes effectively tuning in, context-taking, and recognizing the feelings of others without judgement. Participating in context-taking activities, rehearsing undivided attention, and looking to comprehend assorted perspectives develop compassion and reinforce relational connections.

4. Social abilities: Solid interactive abilities empower people to explore social elements, construct compatibility, and team up successfully. Creating interactive abilities includes rehearsing emphatic correspondence, settling clashes usefully, and encouraging collaboration. Pretending, bunch exercises, and systems administration potentially open doors give roads to levelling up friendly abilities and building a steady informal organisation.

5. Emotional knowledge in administration: In positions of authority, the capacity to understand people at their core is key for rousing and spurring others, encouraging a positive work culture, and driving hierarchical achievement. Pioneers can develop the ability to appreciate people on a deeper level by showing others how it's done, giving useful criticism, and focusing on open correspondence. Establishing a climate that values the ability to understand individuals on a deeper level empowers joint effort, development, and shared regard among colleagues.

6. Continuous learning and development: Improving the ability to appreciate individuals at their core is a continuous excursion that requires devotion and practice. Empowering people to embrace open doors for picking up, looking for criticism, and embracing difficulties cultivates consistent development and advancement. Celebrating progress, recognizing difficulties, and keeping a development mentality add to supported improvement in the capacity to understand people on a profound level.

Taking everything into account, improving the ability to appreciate people on a deeper level is fundamental for individual satisfaction, proficient achievement, and encouraging significant connections. By developing mindfulness, self-guideline, sympathy, interactive abilities, and a guarantee to constant development, people can open their maximum capacity and flourish in all parts of life. Through deliberate practice and a commitment to the capacity to understand people at their core, people can develop satisfying connections, explore difficulties with flexibility, and lead with genuineness and compassion.

Exploring the Role of Emotional Intelligence in Fostering Understanding, Empathy, and Effective Communication Within Marriage

Marriage is a dynamic and complex relationship that requires an elevated degree of the capacity to understand individuals on a profound level to flourish. The capacity to appreciate people on a profound level (EI) assumes an urgent part in encouraging figuring out, sympathy, and compelling correspondence between accomplices. In this top-to-bottom aid, we will investigate how the capacity to appreciate anyone on a profound level adds to the achievement and fulfilment of relationships and gives down-to-earth procedures to upgrade the capacity to understand people at their core inside the setting of marriage.

Figuring out Ability to appreciate anyone on a profound level in Marriage:

1. Self-Awareness: The underpinning of the ability to understand individuals on a deeper level starts with mindfulness. In marriage, mindfulness includes perceiving and grasping one's feelings, triggers, and examples of conduct. Accomplices who are mindful can more readily convey their requirements, wants, and limits, prompting more prominent comprehension and congruity inside the relationship.

2. Self-Regulation: Profound guidelines are fundamental for keeping a solid and amicable marriage. Couples who practise self-guidelines can deal with their feelings successfully, particularly during clashes or conflicts. By remaining even-headed, rehearsing undivided attention, and communicating feelings in a valuable way, accomplices can keep clashes from heightening and track down commonly helpful arrangements.

3. Empathy: Sympathy is the capacity to comprehend and talk about the thoughts of someone else. In marriage, sympathy empowers accomplices to associate on a more profound level, approve of each other's encounters, and deal with support during testing times. Developing sympathy includes undivided attention, viewpoint-taking, and showing veritable worry for your accomplice's prosperity.

4. Effective Communication: Powerful correspondence is the foundation of a sound marriage. The capacity to appreciate people on a deeper level upgrades correspondence by advancing transparency, trustworthiness, and weakness between accomplices. Couples who impart successfully can communicate their necessities and feelings, resolve clashes calmly, and fortify their close-to-home security.

Reasonable Methodologies for Upgrading The ability to understand people at their core in Marriage:

1. Develop Self-Awareness: Urge each other to investigate and think about your feelings, triggers, and correspondence styles. Practice care, journaling, or couples' treatment to develop how you might interpret yourselves and one another.

2. Practice Self-Regulation: Distinguish methods for overseeing pressure, like profound breathing, reflection, or taking a break when clashes emerge. Focus on solid methods for dealing with stress and abstain from falling back on horrendous ways of behaving during snapshots of strain.

3. Cultivate Empathy: Put forth a cognizant attempt to comprehend your accomplice's viewpoint, in any event, when you clash. Practise undivided attention, approve their feelings, and proposition backing and support without judgement or analysis.

4. Improve Correspondence Skills: Learn and rehearse powerful correspondence strategies, like utilising "I" explanations, undivided attention, and nonverbal prompts. Establish a protected and steady climate where the two accomplices feel open to offering their viewpoints, sentiments, and concerns.

5. Seek Proficient Support: Think about looking for couples' treatment or advice to resolve fundamental issues, further develop correspondence, and reinforce your close-to-home security. A prepared specialist can give important bits of knowledge, instruments, and methodologies for improving the capacity to understand individuals at their core and settle clashes usefully.

6. Cultivate a Culture of Appreciation: Offer thanks and appreciation for one another routinely. Commend your victories, support each other through challenges, and focus on quality time together to sustain your profound association.

Taking everything into account, the ability to appreciate people on a deeper level is fundamental for cultivating grasping, compassion, and powerful correspondence inside marriage. By creating mindfulness, rehearsing self-guidelines, developing sympathy, and further developing relational abilities, couples can construct serious areas of strength for a satisfying and thorough organisation. Through continuous responsibility, shared regard, and an eagerness to develop together, couples can fortify their profound bond and explore the intricacies of marriage with flexibility and elegance.

Offering exercises and practices for developing emotional awareness and regulation skills

Close-to-home mindfulness and guidelines are basic parts of the capacity to appreciate individuals on a deeper level, adding to individual prosperity, viable correspondence, and solid connections. In this aid, we will investigate different activities and practices pointed toward creating profound mindfulness and guideline abilities.

1. Care Contemplation:

• Practice: Put away devoted time every day for care reflection. Begin with a couple of moments of centred breathing, continuously expanding the span as you become more agreeable.

• Benefits: Care reflection improves mindfulness by permitting you to notice your considerations, feelings, and substantial sensations without judgment. It likewise advances profound guidelines by developing a feeling of quiet and serenity despite testing feelings.

2. Profound Journaling:

• Practice: Keep a diary where you can record your everyday encounters, considerations, and feelings. Consider huge occasions, triggers, and examples of conduct.

• Benefits: Close-to-home journaling assists you with acquiring an understanding of your profound scene, distinguishing repeating subjects or triggers, and keeping tabs on your development over the long haul. It gives a protected outlet for handling feelings and advancing self-revelation.

3. Body Output Strategy:

• Practice: Participate in a body filter reflection where you methodically center around various pieces of your body, seeing any sensations or pressures present.

• Benefits: The body examination method advances substantial mindfulness, permitting you to perceive how feelings manifest actually in your body. By tuning into substantial sensations, you can all the more likely control your close-to-home reactions and delivery strain or stress.

4. Feeling Naming:

• Practice: Work on naming your feelings as they emerge over the day. Utilize illustrative terms, for example, "delight," "outrage," "bitterness," or "uneasiness" to recognize and recognize what you are feeling.

• Benefits: Feeling naming improves close-to-home mindfulness by carrying clearness and explicitness to your inside encounters. It assists you with knowing between various feelings and answers all the more actually to your necessities and the requirements of others.

5. Breath Mindfulness:

• Practice: Enjoy standard reprieves for the day to zero in on your breath. Notice the vibe of each breathe-in and breathe-out, permitting your breath to secure you right now.

• Benefits: Breath mindfulness fills in as an amazing asset for close-to-home guidelines, assisting you with focusing yourself and tracking down security in fluctuating feelings. By getting back to the breath, you can develop a feeling of quiet and equilibrium in testing circumstances.

6. Moderate Muscle Unwinding (PMR):

• Practice: Take part in moderate muscle unwinding by straining and delivering different muscle bunches in your body consecutively. Begin with your toes and move gradually up to your head.

• Benefits: PMR advances unwinding and lessens physiological excitement related to pressure or nervousness. By deliberately loosening up tense muscles, you can interfere with the pressure reaction and reestablish a feeling of quiet to both body and brain.

7. Appreciation Practice:

• Practice: Develop an everyday appreciation practice by pondering three things you are grateful for every day. Get them on paper or offer them with an accomplice or companion.

• Benefits: Appreciation practice moves your concentration from pessimism to inspiration, cultivating a more adjusted and strong mentality. It advances close-to-home guidelines by developing sensations of happiness, appreciation, and point-of-view taking.

Integrating these activities and practices into your day-to-day schedule can assist you with creating more noteworthy close-to-home mindfulness and guideline abilities after some time. Try different things with various procedures to find what resounds most with you, and recall that consistency and persistence are vital to building the ability to appreciate individuals on a deeper level and prosperity. By supporting your profound mindfulness and guideline abilities, you engage yourself to explore life's difficulties with no sweat, strength, and validness.

Chapter 8:

Strengthening Connection and Intimacy

In the excursion of connections, encouraging association and closeness is fundamental for building areas of strength for getting through connection between accomplices. Section 8 investigates methodologies and practices pointed toward reinforcing association and closeness inside connections, whether heartfelt associations or profound fellowships.

1. Communication Techniques for More Profound Association:

Viable correspondence lies at the core of extending association and closeness. In this section, we dive into strategies like undivided attention, sympathetic correspondence, and weakness. Empowering accomplices to offer their viewpoints, sentiments, and wants transparently encourages shared understanding and fortifies profound association.

2. Building Trust and Weakness:

Trust frames the groundwork of personal connections. This section investigates ways of developing trust through genuineness, dependability, and straightforwardness. Empowering accomplices to rehearse weakness by sharing their feelings of trepidation, instabilities, and desires establishes a protected and strong climate where closeness can thrive.

3. Shared Encounters and Quality Time:

Participating in shared encounters and quality time together reinforces the connection between accomplices. This section investigates exercises like date evenings, shared leisure activities, and significant discussions. Putting investment into supporting the relationship cultivates association and builds up the feeling of organisation and friendship.

4. Exploring Closeness Past Rawness:

Closeness envelops profound, scholarly, and otherworldly association notwithstanding actual closeness. This section urges accomplices to investigate closeness on numerous levels, including profound discussions, shared values, and consistent reassurance. By focusing on close-to-home closeness, accomplices can develop a more profound and seriously satisfying association.

5. Navigating Difficulties and Compromise:

The struggle is a characteristic piece of any relationship, yet the way that accomplices explore difficulties can either reinforce or strain their association. This part investigates procedures for solid compromise, like undivided attention, split the difference, and sympathy. Empowering accomplices to move toward clashes with interest and sympathy cultivates understanding and advances compromise.

6. Cultivating Appreciation and Appreciation:

Offering thanks and appreciation for one another supports the connection among accomplices and upgrades generally relationship fulfilment. This section investigates practices, for example, appreciation journaling, verbal insistence, and thoughtful gestures. Developing a mentality of appreciation cultivates inspiration and reinforces the profound association between accomplices.

7. Embracing Independence and Independence:

While association and closeness are indispensable, accomplices should keep a feeling of distinction and independence. This section investigates the harmony among fellowship and freedom, empowering accomplices to seek after private interests and objectives while additionally supporting the relationship. Regarding each other's independence reinforces common regard and upgrades the nature of the relationship.

Taking everything into account, fortifying association and closeness inside connections requires expectation, exertion, and weakness. By focusing on open correspondence, building trust, putting resources into shared encounters, and exploring difficulties with sympathy and empathy, accomplices can develop a profound and persevering bond. Section 8 gives a guide to encouraging association and closeness, engaging accomplices to construct satisfying and significant connections that endure for the long haul.

Examining the significance of profound and actual closeness in keeping up with closeness and association inside marriage

Profound and actual closeness are fundamental parts of a satisfying and getting through marriage. They structure the groundwork of a profound association between accomplices, cultivating trust, understanding, and shared help. In this aide, we will investigate the meaning of both profound and actual closeness and give bits of knowledge into how couples can support these parts of their relationship to keep up with closeness and association inside marriage.

Grasping Close-to-Home Closeness:

1. Open Correspondence: Close-to-home closeness flourishes with transparent correspondence between accomplices. It includes sharing considerations, sentiments, and weaknesses unafraid of judgement or dismissal.

2. Empathy and Understanding: Profound closeness is developed through compassion and understanding, where accomplices effectively stand by listening to one another's points of view, approve of each other's feelings, and proposition support during critical crossroads.

3. Trust and Weakness: Trust frames the foundation of profound closeness. Accomplices should have a solid sense of security enough to be open to one another, sharing their most profound feelings of trepidation, weaknesses, and dreams without reservation.

Significance of Profound Closeness:

1. Strengthening Association: Profound closeness extends the connection between accomplices, making a feeling of closeness and association that supports the relationship through difficulties and wins.

2. Enhancing Relationship Fulfilment: Couples who focus on profound closeness report more significant levels of relationship fulfilment and in general prosperity. They feel comprehended, esteemed, and upheld by their accomplices, which adds to the more prominent conjugal joy.

3. Navigating Difficulties: Profound closeness furnishes couples with the apparatuses to usefully explore clashes and conflicts. By cultivating compassion and understanding, accomplices can track down commonly gainful arrangements and reinforce their relationship all the while.

Figuring out Actual Closeness:

1. Physical Association: Actual closeness envelops a scope of articulations, including friendly motions, cosy touch, and sexual closeness. It is a strong way for couples to communicate love, want, and warmth for one another.

2. Shared Delight and Closeness: Actual closeness permits accomplices to interface on a sexy and profound level, developing their bond and improving their feelings of closeness and association.

3. Health Advantages: Actual closeness has various medical advantages, including pressure decrease, further developed temperament, and improved resistant capability. It advances by and large prosperity and fortifies the conjugal relationship.

Significance of Actual Closeness:

1. Enhancing Profound Association: Actual closeness supports profound association by encouraging sensations of closeness, warmth, and love between accomplices. It fills in as a substantial articulation of adoration and want, reinforcing the connection between mates.

2. Promoting Relationship Fulfilment: Couples who focus on actual closeness frequently report more elevated levels of relationship fulfilment and conjugal joy. It upgrades sensations of closeness, energy, and sentiment, keeping the flash alive in the relationship.

3. Strengthening Responsibility: Actual closeness is an impression of the responsibility and devotion accomplices have towards one another. It cultivates a feeling of eliteness and organisation, supporting the conjugal bond and extending shared trust and regard.

Sustaining Profound and Actual Closeness:

1. Prioritise Quality Time Together: Put away committed time for significant discussions, shared exercises, and close minutes that reinforce profound and actual association.

2. Communicate Transparently and Truly: Establish a protected and strong climate where the two accomplices feel open to offering their viewpoints, sentiments, and want unafraid of judgement or analysis.

3. Cultivate Trust and Weakness: Cultivate trust and weakness by being straightforward, dependable, and genuinely accessible to one another. Share your deepest considerations, fears, and yearnings, fabricating a groundwork of common comprehension and backing.

4. Celebrate Actual Closeness: Investigate better approaches to communicate actual love and craving for one another. Focus on closeness and delight in your relationship, setting out open doors for shared energy and sentiment.

5. Seek Expert Help if necessary: If close to home or actual closeness is a test in your marriage, think about looking for couples treatment or mentoring. A prepared specialist can give direction, backing, and techniques for improving closeness and association inside your relationship.

All in all, profound and actual closeness are essential parts of a sound and satisfying marriage. By focusing on open correspondence, trust, weakness, and shared actual association, couples can develop a profound and getting-through bond that supports their relationship through life's high points and low points. Putting resources into profound and actual closeness reinforces the underpinning of marriage, cultivating affection, association, and shared satisfaction into the indefinite future.

Giving techniques to extending close-to-home bonds and upgrading closeness through sure cooperation

Constructing and keeping up with close-to-home bonds and closeness is crucial for the well-being and life span of any relationship. Positive communications assume a significant part in sustaining these securities and cultivating a feeling of association between accomplices. In this aid, we will investigate systems and methods for extending profound bonds and upgrading closeness through sure communications inside connections.

1. Focus on Quality Time Together:

• Continuous Consideration: Devote time to associate with your accomplice without interruptions. Take part in exercises you both appreciate and cause each other to feel esteemed and treasured.

• Shared Encounters: Set out open doors for shared encounters and experiences. Travel together, investigate new leisure activities, or appreciate calm snapshots of harmony.

2. Develop Open Correspondence:

• Undivided attention: Practise undivided attention by offering your accomplice your full consideration and approving their contemplations and sentiments. Support open exchange and express veritable interest in their viewpoint.

• Weakness and Credibility: Make a place of refuge for weakness and genuineness. Share your contemplations, fears, and yearnings transparently, and urge your accomplice to do likewise.

3. Express Love and Appreciation:

• Verbal Assertions: Express love, deference, and appreciation for your accomplice through verbal certifications. Praise their assets, commend their accomplishments, and offer thanks for their presence in your life.

• Actual Touch: Actual fondness is a strong method for developing close-to-home bonds and improving closeness. Offer embraces, kisses, and delicate contacts to convey love, solace, and consolation.

4. Practise Sympathy and Understanding:

• Come at the situation from Their Perspective: Develop sympathy by effectively trying to grasp your accomplice's viewpoint and encounters. Approve their feelings and show empathy and backing.

• Approve Sentiments: Approve your accomplice's sentiments regardless of whether you may not completely grasp them. Recognize their feelings and deal with the consolation that you are there to genuinely uphold them.

5. Encourage Perkiness and Chuckling:

• Share Amusing Minutes: Imbue your relationship with humour and liveliness. Share inside jokes, participate in fun-loving chat, and track down chances to chuckle together.

• Make Euphoric Recollections: Search out exercises that give pleasure and chuckling into your relationship. Play prepackaged games, watch comedies, or think back about affectionate recollections to make a cheerful air.

6. Practice Appreciation and Appreciation:

• Offer Thanks: Develop a culture of appreciation by communicating appreciation for your accomplice's presence, commitments, and endeavours. Notice the seemingly insignificant details they do and recognize them with earnestness.

• Appreciation Customs: Integrate appreciation ceremonies into your everyday practice, for example, sharing three things you are thankful for every day or composing love notes communicating your appreciation.

7. Support Each Other's Development and Advancement:

• Empower Self-awareness: Backing your accomplice's objectives, desires, and interests. Urge them to seek after their interests and investigate new open doors for development and improvement.

• Observe Accomplishments: Commend your accomplice's accomplishments and achievements, regardless of how huge or little. Offer consolation, applause, and acknowledgment for their achievements.

8. Focus on Closeness and Association:

• Embrace Actual Closeness: Focus on actual closeness as a method for reinforcing profound bonds and improving association. Investigate each other's longings and inclinations, and focus on shared delight and fulfilment.

• Profound Closeness: Set out open doors for profound association through significant discussions, shared encounters, and thoughtful gestures and backing.

Taking everything into account, developing profound bonds and improving closeness through certain connections requires aim, exertion, and certified care for your accomplice's prosperity. By focusing on quality time together, developing open correspondence, communicating fondness and appreciation, rehearsing sympathy and grasping, cultivating liveliness and giggling, rehearsing appreciation, and supporting each other's development and improvement, you can sustain areas of strength for a getting through association that enhances your relationship and reinforces your security over the long run. Putting resources into positive connections establishes the groundwork for a satisfying and profoundly fulfilling organization based on adoration, trust, and common regard.

Chapter 9:

Fostering Shared Meaning and Purpose

In any significant and satisfying relationship, whether heartfelt or non-romantic, encouraging shared importance and design is fundamental. Part 9 digs into the meaning of developing shared values, objectives, and convictions inside connections and gives systems to support a feeling of shared significance and reason.

1. Defining Shared Importance and Purpose:

Shared importance and reason allude to the aggregate figuring out, values, and objectives that tight spot people together seeing someone. It incorporates shared convictions, customs, and yearnings that give the relationship profundity and importance.

2. Identifying Guiding principle and Beliefs:

This section urges accomplices to investigate and distinguish their guiding principles, convictions, and life needs. By seeing each other's crucial standards and desires, couples can adjust their objectives and activities to create a feeling of a common perspective.

3. Creating Customs and Traditions:

Customs and customs assume a fundamental part in encouraging shared significance and association inside connections. Whether it's celebrating occasions, honoring achievements, or laying out everyday customs, these common encounters fortify the connection among accomplices and support a feeling of having a place and solidarity.

4. Setting Shared Objectives and Aspirations:

Accomplices are urged to define common objectives and desires that mirror their common qualities and vision for what's in store. Whether it's chasing after professional desires, venturing to the far corners of the planet, or beginning a family, having shared objectives gives a feeling of direction and course in the relationship.

5. Navigating Contrasts and Challenges:

While cultivating shared importance and reason, couples might experience contrasts in values, convictions, and needs. This section investigates techniques for exploring these distinctions usefully, encouraging open exchange, splitting the difference, and commonly getting it.

6. Finding Significance in Shared Experiences:

Shared encounters, for example, defeating difficulties, praising victories, and supporting each other through misfortune, add to the feeling of shared importance and reason inside a relationship. By finding significance in these common encounters, couples develop their close-to-home association and flexibility.

7. Communicating Transparently and Authentically:

Successful openness is of the utmost importance for encouraging shared significance and reason. Couples are urged to participate in open, legitimate, and genuine discussions about their qualities, objectives, and yearnings, making an underpinning of trust and understanding.

8. Revisiting and Supporting Shared Meaning:

As connections develop after some time, couples actually must return to and support their common significance and reason. This section gives techniques for intermittently pondering and realigning objectives, values, and desires to guarantee proceeded development and satisfaction.

All in all, encouraging common importance and design is fundamental for developing a profound and satisfying association inside connections. By distinguishing fundamental beliefs, making ceremonies and customs, defining common objectives, exploring contrasts valuably, tracking down significance in shared encounters, conveying straightforwardly and legitimately, and occasionally returning to shared importance, couples can fortify their security and make a relationship that is wealthy in importance, reason, and satisfaction. Section 9 gives a guide to couples to develop a feeling of shared importance and reason, improving their relationship and upgrading their excursion together.

Investigating the idea of shared importance and reason as a wellspring of satisfaction and union in marriage

Marriage is more than a lawful association or a heartfelt association; it is a significant obligation to build a coexistence in light of shared values, objectives, and convictions. Shared importance and reason act as core values that extend the association between accomplices, cultivate flexibility in difficulty, and give a feeling of satisfaction and union inside the marriage. In this aide, we will investigate the idea of shared importance and reason in marriage and give procedures for developing and supporting it.

Grasping Shared Significance and Reason:

1. Shared Qualities and Convictions: Shared importance and reason in marriage are established in like manner values, convictions, and life needs that the two accomplices hold dear. These common establishments give a system of direction, objective setting, and exploring life's difficulties together.

2. Common Objectives and Desires: Couples with shared significance and reason have adjusted objectives and goals for their relationship and their singular lives. Whether it's structuring a family, seeking after vocation desires, or adding to their local area, shared objectives give guidance and inspiration for the marriage.

3. Creating Shared Customs and Customs: Shared importance is much of the time supported through shared ceremonies and customs that hold importance for the couple. These may incorporate praising commemorations, noticing social or strict practices, or laying out day-to-day schedules that fortify the connection between accomplices.

The Significance of Shared Importance and Reason in Marriage:

1. Enhanced Association and Closeness: Shared significance and reason create a feeling of solidarity and association between accomplices, cultivating closeness and profound closeness. Couples who share a typical vision for their lives feel profoundly comprehended and upheld by one another.

2. Resilience Amid Misfortune: During testing times, shared significance and reason give a wellspring of solidarity and strength for couples. Having a common feeling of direction empowers accomplices to weather conditions and storms together, explore vulnerabilities, and arise more grounded from difficulty.

3. Greater Relationship Fulfilment: Couples who offer importance and reason report more significant levels of relationship fulfilment and conjugal bliss. They feel a feeling of satisfaction and reason in their marriage, which adds to by and large prosperity and life fulfilment.

Strategies for Cultivating Shared Meaning and Purpose

1. Open and Fair Correspondence: Encourage transparent correspondence about your qualities, convictions, and goals. Make a place of refuge for sharing your expectations, dreams, and worries with your accomplice.

2. Identify the Guiding principle: Find an opportunity to distinguish and examine your fundamental beliefs and convictions as people and as a couple. Investigate what makes the biggest difference to you and how you can adjust your qualities to make shared significance in your marriage.

3. Set Common Objectives: Cooperatively put forth shared objectives and desires that mirror your common qualities and vision for what's in store. Separate these objectives into significant stages and back each other in accomplishing them.

4. Create Significant Customs and Customs: Lay out ceremonies and customs that hold importance for both of you. Whether it's week-by-week date evenings, yearly getaways, or everyday ceremonies like sharing feasts, these practices support your common association and reason.

5. Navigate Contrasts with Sympathy: Perceive that you and your accomplice might have contrasts in values, convictions, and needs. Move toward these distinctions with sympathy and empathy, looking to see each other's viewpoints and settle on some mutual interest.

6. Celebrate Achievements and Accomplishments: Commend achievements and accomplishments together, recognizing the headway you've made as a couple and the development you've encountered independently. Set aside some margin to offer thanks for one another's commitments to your common process.

7. Revisit and Modify on a case-by-case basis: Intermittently return to your common objectives, values, and desires to guarantee they stay pertinent and significant to both of you. Be available to update and refine your vision for the future as your marriage advances after some time.

All in all shared significance and reason act as the bedrock of a satisfying and strong marriage. By developing open correspondence, recognizing basic beliefs, laying out common objectives, making significant ceremonies, exploring contrasts with empathy, and commending achievements together, couples can extend their association and track down more prominent satisfaction in their common process through life. Putting resources into shared significance and reason reinforces the groundwork of the marriage, giving a wellspring of solidarity, flexibility, and happiness into the indefinite future.

Offering direction on distinguishing and sustaining shared objectives, values, and goals as a team

Building major areas of strength for a satisfying relationship requires something beyond adoration and love; it likewise involves adjusting objectives, values, and yearnings with your accomplice. Distinguishing and supporting shared objectives and values can develop your association, encourage common comprehension, and establish the groundwork for a strong and satisfying organisation. In this aid, we will investigate procedures for distinguishing and supporting shared objectives, values, and desires as a team.

1. Figuring out Shared Objectives, Values, and Yearnings:

1.1 Shared Objectives: Shared objectives are normal goals or results that the two accomplices mean to accomplish together. They can envelop different parts of life, including vocation, family, self-awareness, and way of life decisions.

1.2 Shared Values: Shared values address the standards, convictions, and needs that guide your choices, ways of behaving, and cooperation as a team. They reflect what makes the biggest difference to you both and structure the premise of your common character and vision for what's to come.

1.3 Shared Yearnings: Shared desires are the fantasies, wants, and long-haul objectives that you imagine accomplishing together. They mirror your aggregate expectations for the future and act as a wellspring of inspiration and motivation in your relationship.

2. Methodologies for Recognizing Shared Objectives, Values, and Goals:

2.1 Reflect Independently: Find an opportunity to ponder exclusively your objectives, values, and desires. Consider what satisfies you, what you focus on throughout everyday life, and what you desire to accomplish from here on out.

2.2 Participate in Open Exchange: Encourage transparent correspondence with your accomplice about your qualities, objectives, and desires. Make a safe and non-critical space where you can share your contemplations, sentiments, and dreams uninhibitedly.

2.3 Pose Interesting Inquiries: Offer provocative conversation starters to ignite significant discussions about your common vision for what's in store. For instance:

• What are your most significant qualities and why?

• What do you expect to accomplish exclusively and as a couple in the following five or a decade?

• How would you imagine your optimal way of life, profession, and relational peculiarities?

2.4 Investigate Your Set of Experiences and Foundation: Investigate your singular foundations, childhood, and educational encounters to acquire an understanding of your qualities, convictions, and desires. Talk about how your previous encounters have formed your ongoing viewpoints and objectives.

3. Techniques for Supporting Shared Objectives, Values, and Yearnings:

3.1 Look for Shared belief: Recognize areas of cross-over and arrangement in your objectives, values, and goals. Centre around the qualities and objectives that you both offer and focus on them in your relationship.

3.2 Split the difference and Adaptability: Perceive that you and your accomplice might have contrasts in objectives and values, and split the difference and figure out something worth agreeing on. Practice adaptability and receptiveness to oblige each other's necessities and inclinations.

3.3 Set S.M.A.R.T. Objectives: Set explicit, quantifiable, feasible, applicable, and time-bound (S.M.A.R.T.) objectives that mirror your common goals. Separate bigger objectives into more modest, noteworthy stages to make them more achievable and reasonable.

3.4 Make a Common Vision Board or Plan: Make a visual portrayal of your common objectives, values, and desires utilising a dream board or composed plan. Show it in a conspicuous spot where you can both see it consistently as a sign of your aggregate vision for what's in store.

3.5 Observe Achievements and Accomplishments: Commend achievements and accomplishments together, regardless of how huge or little. Recognize the headway you've made towards your common objectives and offer thanks for one another's commitments to your common process.

3.6 Return to and Modify Routinely: Intermittently return to your common objectives, values, and goals to guarantee they stay significant and significant to both of you. Be available to amend and change your arrangements as your relationship develops and conditions change.

All in all, distinguishing and supporting shared objectives, values, and yearnings as a team is fundamental for building areas of strength, and persevering through relationships. By participating in open exchange, looking for shared views, rehearsing, splitting the difference and adaptability, setting S.M.A.R.T. objectives, making a common vision, praising accomplishments, and returning to and reconsidering consistently, you can fortify your association, extend your comprehension, and make a common future that lines up with your aggregate vision and values. Putting resources into your common objectives and goals establishes the groundwork for a strong and amicable organisation that flourishes over the long haul.

Chapter 10:

Overcoming Challenges and Conflict Resolution

In each relationship, difficulties and clashes are unavoidable. What couples explore these obstructions can altogether mean for the strength and life span of their organisation. Part 10 digs into techniques for conquering difficulties and settling clashes, cultivating grasping, development, and strength inside the relationship.

Grasping Difficulties in Relationships:

1. Variety of Challenges: Difficulties in connections can appear in different structures, including correspondence breakdowns, monetary pressure, contrasts in values, outside tensions, and life advances, for example, being a parent or professional changes.

2. Impact of Challenges: Unsettled difficulties can disintegrate trust, closeness, and association between accomplices, prompting hatred, dissatisfaction, and separation. Tending to difficulties expeditiously and valuably is fundamental for keeping a solid and amicable relationship.

Techniques for Conquering Difficulties and Struggle Resolution:

1. Open and Genuine Communication:

- Encourage transparent correspondence by making a safe and non-critical space for offering viewpoints, sentiments, and concerns.

- Practise undivided attention and sympathy, trying to comprehend your accomplice's point of view before communicating your own.

2. Identify Root Causes:

- Carve out the opportunity to recognize the basic reasons for the difficulties and clashes you're confronting. Look past the surface issues to reveal further feelings, needs, and triggers.

3. Practise Sympathy and Understanding:

- Develop compassion and understanding towards your accomplice's encounters, viewpoints, and feelings. Approve their sentiments and express certified worry for their prosperity.

4. Seek Normal Ground:

- Center around areas of understanding and shared objectives while tending to difficulties and clashes. Recognize shared conviction and work cooperatively towards tracking down commonly OK arrangements.

5. Use "I" Proclamations and Stay away from Blame:

- Use "I" proclamations to offer your viewpoints, sentiments, and necessities without allocating fault or analysis to your accomplice. Centre around articulating your thoughts decisively and valuably.

6. Develop Compromise Skills:

- Learn and rehearse viable compromise abilities, for example, undivided attention, critical thinking, splitting the difference, and exchanging. Move toward clashes as any open doors for development and understanding.

7. Take Obligation and Apologise When Necessary:

- Assume a sense of ownership with your activities and recognize the effect they might have had on your accomplice. Offer certifiable conciliatory sentiments while required, communicating regret and a guarantee to positive change.

8. Take Breaks When Necessary:

- If feelings arise during clashes, enjoy some time off to chill and recover. Put down a point in time to return to the discussion once the two accomplices feel more settled and more gathered.

9. Seek Backing When Needed:

- Consider looking for help from a couples' specialist or instructor while confronting critical difficulties or repeating clashes. A prepared proficient can give direction, viewpoint, and instruments for settling clashes helpfully.

10. Focus on Arrangements, Not Winning:

- Move toward clashes with a cooperative mentality, zeroing in on finding arrangements that benefit the two accomplices as opposed to winning or being "correct." Focus on the well-being and prosperity of the relationship above individual self-images.

All in all, conquering difficulties and settling clashes is a fundamental part of keeping a sound and flourishing relationship. By cultivating open correspondence, sympathy, and understanding, recognizing underlying drivers, looking for a shared belief, rehearsing compromise abilities, assuming liability, and looking for help when required, couples can explore difficulties with elegance and strength. Section 10 gives important bits of knowledge and techniques for beating obstructions, cultivating development, and reinforcing the connection between accomplices, eventually making a relationship that twists despite misfortune.

Discussing common challenges and sources of conflict in marriage

Marriage is an excursion overflowing with delights, wins, and shared encounters, yet it is likewise joined by difficulties and clashes that can test the strength and flexibility of the relationship. Understanding normal difficulties and wellsprings of contention in marriage is fundamental for couples to explore these snags successfully and fabricate areas of strength for an organisation. In this aid, we will investigate the absolute most predominant difficulties and wellsprings of contention in marriage and give bits of knowledge into how couples can address them productively.

1. Correspondence Breakdown:

• Issue: Unfortunate correspondence or miscommunication can prompt errors, disappointment, and hatred between accomplices.

• Underlying drivers: Contrasts in correspondence styles, absence of undivided attention, and unexpressed requirements or assumptions.

• Influence: Correspondence breakdowns can disintegrate trust, closeness, and association in the marriage.

2. Monetary Pressure:

• Issue: Monetary difficulties, obligations, or conflicts about cash the executives can put pressure on and strain the marriage.

• Underlying drivers: Contrasts in monetary qualities, ways of managing money, or monetary objectives.

• Influence: Monetary pressure can prompt contentions, uneasiness, and sensations of uncertainty inside the relationship.

3. Adjusting Work and Day to day Life:

• Issue: Tracking down a harmony between work liabilities, family commitments, and individual time can be trying for couples.

• Underlying drivers: Clashing needs, requesting work timetables, and trouble defining limits.

• Influence: Irregularity in work-life elements can prompt sensations of disregard, hatred, and burnout.

4. Contrasts in Nurturing Styles:

• Issue: Conflicts about nurturing approaches, discipline, and youngster-raising choices can strain the marriage.

• Underlying drivers: Changed childhood, social contrasts, and clashing convictions about nurturing.

• Influence: Contrasts in nurturing styles can prompt strain, contentions, and difficulties in co-nurturing.

5. Closeness and Sexual Issues:

• Issue: Diminished closeness, crisscrossed charisma, or irritating sexual issues can create distance and disappointment in the marriage.

• Underlying drivers: Stress, weakness, annoying intense subject matters, and changes in physical or close-to-home wellbeing.

• Influence: Closeness and sexual issues can prompt sensations of dismissal, dissatisfaction, and detachment between accomplices.

6. Outside Stressors and Life Advances:

• Issue: Life advances, for example, migration, profession changes, disease, or misfortune can overwhelm the marriage.

• Main drivers: Change challenges, vulnerability, and expanded liabilities during seasons of progress.

• Influence: Outside stressors can enhance existing strains and make it extra difficult for the couple to explore.

7. Contrasts in Values and Convictions:

• Issue: Clashing qualities, convictions, and needs can prompt conflicts and difficulties in direction.

• Main drivers: Social contrasts, strict convictions, and individual encounters that shape individual viewpoints.

• Influence: Contrasts in values and convictions can cause division and strife inside the marriage if not tended to really.

8. Absence of Value Time Together:

• Issue: Occupied plans, contending needs, and outside responsibilities can restrict amazing open doors for quality time and association.

• Underlying drivers: Overcommitment, absence of prioritisation, and trouble in adjusting individual and couple time.

• Influence: Absence of value time together can prompt sensations of depression, disengagement, and disregard in the marriage.

Tending to Normal Difficulties and Wellsprings of Contention:

1. Open and Legit Correspondence: Cultivate open exchange, undivided attention, and compassion to resolve hidden issues and concerns successfully.

2. Seeking Expert Help: Think about couples' treatment or guidance to acquire knowledge, points of view, and apparatuses for exploring difficulties and clashes productively.

3. Compromise and Cooperation: Practise splitting the difference, adaptability, and joint effort while tending to contrasts and tracking down commonly adequate arrangements.

4. Prioritising Relationship Support: Put forth purposeful attempts to focus on the well-being and prosperity of the relationship through ordinary registrations, quality time together, and shared exercises.

5. Cultivating Compassion and Figuring out: Cultivate sympathy and understanding towards your accomplice's encounters, points of view, and feelings to fortify association and encourage common help.

Taking everything into account, while difficulties and clashes are an unavoidable piece of marriage, they likewise present open doors for development, understanding, and association between accomplices. By recognizing normal wellsprings of contention, cultivating open correspondence, looking for help when required, and focusing on the well-being and prosperity of the relationship, couples can explore difficulties successfully and fabricate areas of strength for an organisation that endures everyday hardship.

Introducing positive conflict resolution strategies and techniques for fostering understanding and compromise

Struggle is a characteristic and inescapable part of any relationship, including marriage. What couples explore clashes can significantly mean for the well-being and life span of their association. Positive compromise techniques enable couples to address conflicts usefully, encouraging grasping, compassion, and splitting the difference. In this aid, we will investigate powerful strategies for settling clashes in a sound and useful way.

1. Cultivate Open Correspondence:

1.1 Undivided attention: Practise undivided attention by concentrating on your accomplice's point of view without intruding on or planning a reaction. Approve their sentiments and look to figure out their perspective.

1.2 Use "I" Proclamations: Offer your viewpoints, sentiments, and concerns utilising "I" explanations to take responsibility for feelings without appointing fault or analysis to your accomplice.

2. Develop Compassion and Understanding:

2.1 Come at the situation from Their Perspective: Develop compassion by envisioning yourself in your accomplice's situation. Think about their sentiments, needs, and encounters to acquire a more profound comprehension of their point of view.

2.2 Approve Their Sentiments: Approve your accomplice's sentiments and encounters, regardless of whether you may not concur with their point of view. Recognize the legitimacy of their feelings and show sympathy and empathy.

3. Practice Self-assured Correspondence:

3.1 Express Your Requirements Obviously: Articulate your necessities, concerns, and limits in a deferential and self-assured way. Utilise emphatic correspondence methods to put yourself out there unhesitatingly without depending on animosity or antagonism.

3.2 Keep away from Protectiveness and Fault: Avoid becoming guarded or turning to fault during clashes. Centre around resolving the main thing cooperatively as opposed to taking part in private assaults or analyses.

4. Look for Shared conviction:

4.1 Distinguish Shared Objectives: Spotlight on areas of understanding and shared objectives while looking for goals. Underline the common qualities and desires that join you as a team.

4.2 Split the difference and Adaptability: split the difference and find intelligent fixes that oblige the two accomplices' requirements and inclinations. Practice adaptability and receptiveness to elective points of view.

5. Take Breaks When Required:

5.1 Perceive Raising Feelings: Focus on indications of heightened feelings, like uplifted strain or dissatisfaction. If clashes become excessively warmed, consider taking a break to chill and recover.

5.2 Settle on Standard procedures: Layout guidelines for breaks, for example, a foreordained term and a pledge to get back to the discussion whenever feelings have settled.

6. Practise Critical thinking Abilities:

6.1 Characterise the Issue: Characterise the main thing in need of attention and distinguish the hidden causes adding to the contention. Separate the issue into sensible parts to work with critical thinking.

6.2 Talk Arrangements: Create a scope of potential arrangements together, taking into account the upsides and downsides of every choice. Be imaginative and liberal in investigating elective ways to deal with goals.

7. Centre around the Issue, Not the Individual:

7.1 Separate Among Conduct and Individual: Recognize the particular way of behaving or issue causing the contention and the actual individual. Abstain from making summed up or individual assaults during conflicts.

7.2 Keep up With Deference and Politeness: Approach your join forces with deference and mutual respect, in any event, during snapshots of conflict. Practice benevolence, persistence, and grasping in your collaborations.

8. Reflect and Gain from Clashes:

8.1 Think about Struggle Examples: Find an opportunity to consider repeating struggle designs and basic elements inside your relationship. Recognize normal triggers and examples to proactively address fundamental issues.

8.2 Gain from Struggle Encounters: View clashes as any open doors for development and advancement inside your relationship. Remove important experiences and examples from past struggles to illuminate future connections.

9. Look for Help When Required:

9.1 Think about Couples Treatment: If clashes endure or become overpowering, think about looking for help from a couples specialist or guide. A prepared proficient can give direction, viewpoint, and instruments for exploring clashes valuably.

9.2 Take part in Relationship Training: Take part in relationship schooling projects or studios pointed toward upgrading relational abilities, compromise methods, and relationship fulfilment.

Taking everything into account, positive compromise systems are fundamental for encouraging grasping, sympathy, and splitting the differences inside marriage. By encouraging open correspondence, developing sympathy and understanding, rehearsing confident correspondence, looking for shared conviction, taking breaks while required, rehearsing critical thinking abilities, zeroing in on the issue, considering struggle encounters, and looking for help when required, couples can explore clashes usefully and reinforce their relationship simultaneously. Putting resources into positive compromise methods establishes the groundwork for a versatile, amicable, and satisfying organisation that flourishes notwithstanding difficulties.

Chapter 11:

Cultivating Joy and Playfulness

In the excursion of marriage, amid everyday obligations and difficulties, couples must sustain delight and perkiness inside their relationship. Part 11 investigates the meaning of developing happiness and liveliness and gives methodologies to inject merriment and giggling into the conjugal bond.

Grasping the Significance of Bliss and Playfulness:

1. Stress Reduction: Delight and fun-loving nature act as strong counteractants to stretch, assisting couples with easing pressure and cultivating close-to-home prosperity.

2. Enhanced Connection: Divided chuckling and lively associations reinforce the profound association among accomplices, extending closeness and common comprehension.

3. Promotion of Resilience: Developing delight and liveliness improves strength inside the relationship, empowering couples to explore difficulties with confidence and energy.

Procedures for Developing Delight and Playfulness:

1. Prioritise Quality Time Together:

- Put away devoted time for shared exercises and encounters that give pleasure and giggling. Take part in leisure activities, trips, or experiences that permit you to associate and have a good time together.

2. Embrace Suddenness and Creativity:

- Embrace suddenness by consolidating shock motions, unconstrained excursions, or perky amazements into your relationship. Encourage imagination by investigating new exercises or leisure activities together.

3. Infuse Humor into Everyday Life:

- Develop a funny bone by tracking down open doors for good cheer and giggling in regular minutes. Share jokes, entertaining stories, or lively exchanges to create a positive and inspiring environment.

4. Engage in Energetic Interactions:

- Integrate energetic cooperation into your everyday daily practice, like lively prodding, delicate actual touch, or fun-loving difficulties. Move toward errands and obligations with a feeling of liveliness and collaboration.

5. Explore Novel Encounters Together:

- Step beyond your usual range of familiarity and investigate novel encounters together, whether it's difficult new exercises, investigating new objections, or leaving on unconstrained undertakings.

6. Celebrate Achievements and Achievements:

- Commend achievements, accomplishments, and exceptional minutes along with excitement and happiness. Recognize and value each other's triumphs, regardless of how little.

7. Practice Appreciation and Appreciation:

- Develop a culture of appreciation by communicating appreciation for one another's presence, commitments, and characteristics. Routinely offer thanks for the delight and energy your accomplice brings into your life.

8. Create Ceremonies of Connection:

- Lay out ceremonies of association that cultivate euphoria and perkiness inside your relationship. Whether it's a week-after-week game evening, a month-to-month experience, or an everyday snapshot of giggling, focus on these ceremonies as a wellspring of euphoria and association.

9. Maintain a Positive Mindset:

- Develop a positive outlook by zeroing in on the positive qualities in one another and your relationship. Move toward difficulties with positive thinking and flexibility, perceiving that bliss can be tracked down even in troublesome times.

10. Encourage Honest Wonder:

- Embrace the soul of honest miracle and interest by moving toward existence with a feeling of stunningness and appreciation. Track down satisfaction in the straightforward delights of day-to-day existence and urge each other to embrace miracles and interest.

All in all, developing euphoria and perkiness inside a marriage is fundamental for sustaining profound association, strength, and prosperity. By focusing on quality time together, embracing immediacy and imagination, implanting humour into day-to-day existence, taking part in lively collaborations, investigating novel encounters, praising achievements, rehearsing appreciation and appreciation, making ceremonies of association, keeping a positive mentality, and empowering honest miracle, couples can mix their relationship with euphoria, chuckling, and essentialness. Putting resources into the development of euphoria and energy establishes the groundwork for an energetic, satisfying, and persevering organisation that flourishes with adoration, chuckling, and common joy.

Highlighting the importance of laughter, play, and spontaneity in nurturing marital happiness

Giggling, play, and immediacy are fundamental fixings in developing a cheerful and satisfying marriage. They implant associations with euphoria, daintiness, and a feeling of association that fortifies the connection between accomplices. In this aide, we'll investigate why giggling, play, and immediacy are essential parts of conjugal satisfaction and give techniques for integrating them into your relationship.

1. The Force of Giggling:

1.1 Pressure Alleviation: Chuckling is a characteristic pressure reliever that assists couples with exploring difficulties and mishaps with strength and hopefulness.

1.2 Improved Profound Association: Divided giggling cultivates close-to-home closeness and extends the association among accomplices, creating a feeling of kinship and shared understanding.

1.3 Advancement of Inspiration: Chuckling advances an uplifting perspective on life and urges couples to move toward troubles with humour and merriment.

2. The Job of Play:

2.1 Holding and Association: Energetic communications reinforce the connection between accomplices by cultivating a feeling of shared bliss and experience.

2.2 Arrival of Strain: Play gives an outlet to delivering pressure and repressed energy, making a loose and charming climate inside the relationship.

2.3 Cultivating Inventiveness and Development: Play empowers innovativeness and advancement, permitting couples to investigate novel thoughts and encounters together.

3. Embracing Immediacy:

3.1 Rediscovering Energy: Immediacy infuses fervour and oddity into the relationship, keeping the flash alive and reigniting enthusiasm after some time.

3.2 Upgraded Closeness: Unconstrained tokens of love and shock extend closeness and reaffirm the association between accomplices.

3.3 Development of Experience: Embracing immediacy urges couples to embrace the experience and embrace life's shocks with open hearts and brains.

Techniques for Integrating Chuckling, Play, and Immediacy:

1. Schedule Normal Recess: Put away committed time for energetic exercises, for example, tabletop games, open-air experiences, or inventive activities, to reconnect and bond with your accomplice.

2. Infuse Humor into day-to-day existence: Track down potential open doors for giggling and merriment in regular minutes by sharing jokes, entertaining stories, or energetic chit chat with your accomplice.

3. Embrace Unconstrained Experiences: Immediately jump all over unconstrained chances for experience and investigation, whether it's difficult for another café, setting out on an unconstrained excursion, or taking a dance class together.

4. Create Customs of Association: Lay out ceremonies of association that focus on chuckling, play, and suddenness, like a week-after-week film night, a month-to-month night out on the town, or an unconstrained excursion in the recreation area.

5. Practice Fun-loving Correspondence: Consolidate perky correspondence strategies, like utilising humour, mind, and friendly prodding, to ease up the temperament and encourage closeness in your communications.

6. Step External Your Usual range of familiarity: Challenge yourselves to step outside your usual range of familiarity and attempt new exercises or encounters together that light fervour and happiness.

7. Celebrate Achievements with Happiness: Commend achievements, accomplishments, and extraordinary minutes with energy and bliss, making enduring recollections that reinforce your security as a team.

8. Stay Present and Careful: Develop care and presence in your relationship by enjoying the experience and valuing the delight and excellence that encompasses you.

All in all, giggling, play, and immediacy are essential parts of conjugal joy, encouraging bliss, association, and closeness inside connections. By focusing on valuable open doors for chuckling, embracing energetic connections, and embracing suddenness, couples can make a dynamic and satisfying organisation that blossoms with shared encounters and common joy. Putting resources into chuckling, play, and immediacy improves the excursion of marriage, injecting it with a feeling of experience, wonder, and unlimited satisfaction.

Offering suggestions for incorporating joy and playfulness into daily interactions and shared experiences

Mixing delight and perkiness into everyday cooperation and shared encounters is a strong method for developing satisfaction and extending close-to-home association inside a relationship. By embracing snapshots of giggling, immediacy, and happiness, couples can make an energetic and satisfying organisation that blossoms with shared satisfaction and inspiration. In this aid, we'll investigate commonsense ideas for integrating delight and perkiness into day-to-day existence as a team.

1. Begin Your Day with Inspiration:

1.1 Wake-up routines: Start every day with a positive wake-up routine, like sharing some espresso or tea, trading uplifting statements, or participating in a carefree exchange to establish a cheerful vibe for the day ahead.

1.2 Offer Thanks: Pause for a minute every morning to offer thanks for each other and the endowments in your lives. Developing an outlook of appreciation makes way for a day overflowing with delight and appreciation.

2. Implant Humor into Everyday Communications:

2.1 Offer Interesting Stories: Offer entertaining tales or amusing stories from your day to bring giggling and gentility into your discussions. Find humor in the ordinary minutes and embrace the ridiculousness of coexistence.

2.2 Utilise Lively Correspondence: Integrate fun-loving correspondence methods, like clever chitchat, inside jokes, or energetic prodding, to mix your cooperation with giggling and immediacy. Partake in the lively trade of loving chat and humor.

3. Integrate Lively Exercises into Everyday Daily schedule:

3.1 Dance Gatherings: Have extemporaneous dance parties in the family room to your main tunes or make a playlist of peppy tunes to give you a much-needed boost and stimulate your day.

3.2 Table games and Riddles: Put away opportunities for tabletop games, riddles, or games that energise chuckling, agreeable rivalry, and shared satisfaction. Embrace the soul of play and experience together.

4. Embrace Unconstrained Experiences:

4.1 Investigate Your Environmental Factors: Go for unconstrained strolls or drives together to investigate new areas, parks, or picturesque spots in your space. Embrace the feeling of experience and disclosure that accompanies investigating the world together.

4.2 Attempt New Exercises: Step beyond your usual range of familiarity and attempt new exercises or side interests together, whether it's cooking another recipe, learning a dance schedule, or taking a composition class. Embrace the delight of learning and disclosure as a team.

5. Make Ceremonies of Association:

5.1 Week after Week Date Evenings: Timetable normal date evenings to reconnect and bond as a team. Whether it's a heartfelt supper, a film night at home, or a dusk walk, focus on quality time together to sustain your relationship.

5.2 Family Fun Days: Plan a family fun day or excursion with your youngsters to make treasured recollections and fortify family bonds. Participate in lively exercises, like picnics, outside games, or imaginative expressions and specialties projects.

6. Observe Achievements and Accomplishments:

6.1 Observe Little Triumphs: Recognize and commend each other's achievements, regardless of how little. Whether it's a work accomplishment, an individual achievement, or a common achievement, carve out opportunities to gather together to celebrate and communicate pride in one another's achievements.

6.2 Make Customs of Festivity: Lay out ceremonies of festivity for exceptional events, commemorations, and achievements in your relationship. Whether it's a candlelit supper, an end-of-the-week escape, or a sincere toast, make every festival paramount and significant.

7. Remain Present and Careful:

7.1 Enjoy the Experience: Practice care and presence in your everyday associations by relishing the experience and valuing the delight and excellence that encompasses you. Be completely present with one another and treasure the straightforward joys of coexistence.

7.2 Track down Delight in Regular Minutes: Embrace the magnificence of the normal and track down euphoria in ordinary snapshots of association and harmony. Whether it's sharing a dinner, watching the nightfall, or snuggling on the sofa, love these snapshots of closeness and delight.

In conclusion, Integrating euphoria and energy into everyday communications and shared encounters is fundamental for sustaining a cheerful and satisfying relationship. By beginning every day with energy, injecting humour into day-to-day communications, integrating perky exercises into your daily practice, embracing unconstrained experiences, making customs of association, commending achievements and accomplishments, and remaining present and careful, couples can develop a relationship loaded up with chuckling, love, and euphoria. Putting resources into delightful and fun-loving nature enhances the texture of your relationship, creating a common feeling of satisfaction and satisfaction that supports you through life's promising and less promising times.

Chapter 12: Sustaining Growth and Renewal

In the last section of your conjugal excursion, supporting development and reestablishment becomes central to the lifespan and essentialness of your relationship. Section 12 spotlights techniques and ways to deal with keep supporting your marriage, encouraging individual and social development, and embracing recharging to guarantee your organisation stays solid and dynamic.

Figuring out the Requirement for Development and Renewal:

1. Dynamic Nature of Relationships: Perceive that connections advance over the long run, and supporting development and reestablishment is fundamental for keeping your marriage dynamic and versatile.

2. Preventing Stagnation: Without purposeful exertion, connections can deteriorate, prompting smugness and detachment. Supporting development and reestablishment forestalls stagnation and keeps the relationship alive and flourishing.

3. Adapting to Life Changes: Life is loaded up with changes, both expected and startling. Supporting development and reestablishment prepares couples to adjust to these progressions together, reinforcing their bond and versatility.

Systems for Supporting Development and Renewal:

1. Commit to Deep rooted Learning:

- Embrace a mentality of long-lasting learning, both independently and as a couple. Put resources into self-improvement through perusing, going to studios, or seeking leisure activities and interests.

2. Prioritise Correspondence and Connection:

- Keep up with transparent correspondence with your accomplice, consistently monitoring each other's necessities, wants, and yearnings. Focus on quality time together to sustain close-to-home association and closeness.

3. Set and Seek after Shared Goals:

- Cooperatively put forth and seek after shared objectives as a team, whether they are connected with vocation, family, self-improvement, or travel. Making progress toward normal goals cultivates a feeling of solidarity and reason in the relationship.

4. Embrace Novel Experiences:

- Embrace curiosity and experience by searching out new encounters together. Investigate new side interests, travel to new objections, or challenge yourselves with energising exercises that light enthusiasm and interest.

5. Practice Appreciation and Appreciation:

- Develop a culture of appreciation by routinely communicating appreciation for your accomplice and the endowments in your day-to-day existence. Commend each other's assets, accomplishments, and commitments to the relationship.

6. Engage in Normal Reflection:

- Put away opportunities for ordinary reflection as a team to evaluate the well-being and direction of your relationship. Ponder your development as people and as accomplices, distinguishing regions for development and praising achievements.

7. Embrace Change and Adaptability:

- Embrace change as a characteristic piece of life and connections. Adjust to new conditions, jobs, and difficulties with adaptability, flexibility, and a feeling of joint effort.

8. Seek Backing and Guidance:

- Make it a point to seek help and direction from confided-in companions, relatives, or expert guides while confronting critical difficulties or changes in your relationship. A new point of view can give clearness and understanding.

9. Celebrate Your Affection and Commitment:

- Commend your affection and obligation to one another routinely. Whether it's through heartfelt emotions, ardent discussions, or extraordinary ceremonies, track down significant ways of respecting your relationship and reaffirming your bond.

All in all, supporting development and restoration in marriage is a continuous excursion that requires devotion, deliberateness, and shared exertion. By focusing on deep-rooted picking up, focusing on correspondence and association, putting forth and chasing after shared objectives, embracing novel encounters, rehearsing appreciation and appreciation, participating in normal reflection, embracing change and flexibility, looking for help and direction, and praising your adoration and responsibility, you can guarantee that your relationship proceeds to thrive and develop after some time. Recollect that supporting development and recharging isn't just about saving the state of affairs but about effectively putting resources into the eventual fate of your organisation, making a tradition of affection, flexibility, and satisfaction that endures forever.

Talking about the idea of deep-rooted learning and development inside marriage

Long-lasting learning and development in marriage are fundamental parts of a solid and satisfying organisation. Embracing the idea of constant learning and self-improvement fortifies the connection between accomplices, encourages shared understanding, and advances strength despite life's difficulties. In this aide, we'll dive into the meaning of deep-rooted learning and development inside marriage and investigate techniques for coordinating this idea into your relationship.

Figuring out Deep rooted Learning and Development:

1. Continuous Self-improvement:

• Deep-rooted learning includes a promise to self-improvement, self-revelation, and constant improvement all through one's life.

• Inside marriage, deep-rooted learning includes the ability of the two accomplices to advance, gain from encounters, and take a stab at individual satisfaction and self-realisation.

2. Adapting to Change and Difficulties:

• Long-lasting acquiring outfits coupled with the abilities and versatility expected to explore life's advances, difficulties, and vulnerabilities.

• By embracing development and learning, couples can adjust to evolving conditions, jobs, and obligations inside their relationship and more extensive life settings.

3. Fostering Ability to appreciate individuals on a deeper level and Sympathy:

• Long-lasting learning advances the improvement of the capacity to appreciate individuals on a profound level and sympathy, empowering couples to impart successfully, resolve clashes valuably, and sustain understanding and empathy towards one another.

Strategies for Integrating Lifelong Learning and Growth Into Marriage

1. Create a Culture of Interest:

• Cultivate a culture of interest and investigation inside your marriage by empowering receptiveness, scholarly interest, and a hunger for information.

• Investigate new interests, leisure activities, and encounters together, starting discussions and shared disclosures that advance your relationship.

2. Set Individual and Shared Objectives:

• Urge each other to put forth private and shared objectives that line up with your singular qualities, interests, and goals.

• Routinely return to your objectives as a team, commending accomplishments, reconsidering needs, and changing your direction depending on the situation to help each other's development and satisfaction.

3. Prioritise Correspondence and Reflection:

• Set out open doors for significant correspondence and reflection inside your relationship. Put away opportunities for fair discussions about your expectations, fears, dreams, and difficulties.

• Practise undivided attention, compassion, and weakness, establishing a protected and steady climate where the two accomplices feel esteemed and comprehended.

4. Seek Learning Open doors Together:

• Investigate open doors for joint mastering and ability-building exercises, like going to studios, signing up for classes, or setting out on instructive experiences.

• Embrace the method involved with learning together, commending each other's advancement, and sharing experiences acquired en route.

5. Embrace Criticism and Development Outlook:

• Embrace criticism as an instrument for development and improvement inside your marriage. Move toward useful analysis with a receptive outlook and a development mentality, seeing difficulties as any open doors for learning and improvement.

• Give strong criticism to your accomplice, offering support, direction, and productive ideas for individual and social development.

6. Celebrate Achievements and Progress:

• Commend achievements, accomplishments, and snapshots of self-improvement inside your marriage. Recognize the headway you've made exclusively and as a couple, offer thanks for the excursion you've shared.

7. Cultivate a Feeling of Flexibility:

• Develop flexibility as a team by embracing the certainty of difficulties, disappointments, and disillusionments as any open doors for learning and development.

• Move toward difficulties with idealism, cleverness, and a common obligation to beat snags together, drawing strength from the profundity of your association and shared help.

All in all, long-lasting learning and development inside marriage structure the underpinning of a dynamic, strong, and satisfying organisation. By embracing the idea of consistent picking up, encouraging individual and shared development, focusing on correspondence and reflection, looking for learning potential open doors together, embracing input and a development mentality, commending achievements and progress, and developing a feeling of flexibility, couples can explore the intricacies of hitched existence with elegance, insight, and common regard. Embrace the excursion of long-lasting advancing inside your marriage, perceiving that the quest for development and self-disclosure isn't just a pathway to individual satisfaction yet in addition a wellspring of significant association and closeness inside your relationship.

Giving direction on embracing change, looking for new encounters, and recharging the conjugal bond after some time

Change is inescapable, and as a couple, embracing change, looking for new encounters, and recharging the conjugal bond over the long run is fundamental for supporting a sound, lively relationship. In this aid, we'll investigate the significance of embracing change, looking for new encounters, and recharging the conjugal bond, alongside pragmatic direction for integrating these components into your marriage.

Figuring out the Significance of Embracing Change and Looking for New Encounters:

1. Fostering Development and Versatility:

• Embracing change encourages individual and social development, empowering couples to adjust to new conditions, jobs, and difficulties as they emerge.

• Looking for new encounters strengthens the relationship, starting interest, energy, and a feeling of shared experience.

2. Preventing Stagnation and Carelessness:

• Embracing change and looking for new encounters forestall stagnation and carelessness inside the relationship, keeping the conjugal bond dynamic and tough.

• Routine and commonality can prompt weariness and detachment, while oddity and investigation reignite energy and interest.

Direction on Embracing Change, Looking for New Encounters, and Reestablishing the Conjugal Bond:

1. Cultivate Open Correspondence:

• Encourage transparent correspondence with your accomplice about your cravings, goals, and fears concerning change and new encounters.

• Make a protected and strong space where the two accomplices feel enabled to offer their viewpoints, concerns, and dreams.

2. Embrace a Development Mentality:

• Embrace a development mentality that invites change as a chance for learning, self-revelation, and self-improvement.

• View difficulties as any open doors for development and change, moving toward them with strength, confidence, and a readiness to adjust.

3. Step External Your Usual range of familiarity:

• Challenge yourselves to step outside your usual range of familiarity and investigate new encounters together. Whether it's going to new objections, attempting new exercises, or meeting new individuals, embrace the experience of the unexplored world.

• Urge each other to embrace weakness and vulnerability, confiding in your common strength and versatility to explore new territory.

4. Prioritise Shared Encounters:

• Focus on shared encounters and experiences that extend your association and make enduring recollections. Whether it's investigating nature, going to widespread developments, or setting out on unconstrained excursions, focus on quality time together.

• Make customs and customs that honour your common qualities and yearnings, reaffirming your obligation to one another and the excursion of development and recharging.

5. Celebrate Achievements and Ponder Your Excursion:

• Commend achievements and accomplishments in your relationship, finding an opportunity to ponder your excursion together and offer thanks for the development and change you've encountered.

• Consider the difficulties you've survived, the examples you've learned, and the snapshots of euphoria and association that have supported you en route.

6. Seek Oddity and Imagination in Day to day existence:

• Inject curiosity and innovativeness into your day-to-day existence by trying different things with new schedules, exercises, and customs.

• Embrace suddenness and perkiness, permitting yourselves to be motivated by the excellence and marvel of your general surroundings.

7. Support Each Other's Self-improvement:

• Support each other's self-improvement and individual pursuits, praising each other's accomplishments and achievements.

• Urge each other to seek after interests, side interests, and interests that carry satisfaction and importance to your lives, encouraging a feeling of independence and individual organisation inside the relationship.

Embracing change, looking for new encounters, and re-establishing the conjugal bond over the long haul are fundamental for supporting a dynamic and satisfying relationship. By developing open correspondence, embracing a development mentality, venturing outside your usual range of familiarity, focusing on shared encounters, commending achievements, looking for oddity and inventiveness, and supporting each other's self-improvement, you can make a marriage that blossoms with experience, disclosure, and common regard. Embrace the excursion of development and reestablishment, perceiving that change isn't just unavoidable yet in addition a chance for more profound association, closeness, and euphoria inside your relationship.

Conclusion

As we close our investigation of "Harmony in Hearts: Positive Psychology Practices for Lasting Marriages," it is obvious that the excursion of marriage is a powerful embroidery woven with strings of adoration, strength, and development. All through these pages, we've dug into the primary standards of positive brain science and its groundbreaking effect on conjugal prosperity.

Chasing enduring amicability, we've uncovered the meaning of encouraging the capacity to appreciate anyone on a deeper level, supporting sympathy, and developing powerful correspondence inside the conjugal association. We've investigated the significant significance of profound and actual closeness, the force of shared importance and reason, and the need to embrace difficulties with effortlessness and understanding. From upgrading profound attention to developing associations through certain communications, from cultivating delight and fun-loving nature to embracing change and looking for restoration, the practices illustrated in this book act as directing signals for couples exploring the intricacies of hitched life.

As you leave on your excursion together, may you find comfort in the ageless insight shared inside these pages. May you embrace every second with appreciation and receptiveness, perceiving the magnificence and likely inbornness in each common experience. Keep in mind, that the way to enduring amiability isn't without its exciting bends in the road, however, it is enlightened by getting through light of affection and responsibility. With devotion, empathy, and unflinching faith in the groundbreaking force of positive brain science, may your hearts keep on reverberating as a unified whole, presently and for every one of the days to come.

Here's to a lifetime loaded up with adoration, chuckling, and the steadfast quest for concordance in your souls.

Summing up key bits of knowledge and practices for developing a thriving marriage through sure brain research standards

Developing a thriving marriage through certain brain research standards includes embracing key experiences and practices that feed close-to-home association, strength, and development inside the relationship. Here is an outline of key bits of knowledge and practices:

1. Emotional Intelligence: Develop the ability to appreciate people at their core by creating mindfulness and compassion. Comprehend and deal with your feelings while being receptive to your accomplice's sentiments and requirements.

2. Effective Communication: Practise undivided attention, sympathy, and confident correspondence. Encourage transparent discourse, permitting space for approval, understanding, and goal of contentions.

3. Empathy and Understanding: Sustain sympathy and grasping inside the relationship. Relate to your accomplice's encounters, points of view, and feelings, cultivating a feeling of common help and approval.

4. Emotional and Actual Intimacy: Focus on close to home and actual closeness, encouraging association, trust, and warmth. Set out open doors for significant association and closeness, sustaining the connection between accomplices.

5. Shared Meaning and Purpose: Distinguish and sustain shared objectives, values, and yearnings. Develop a feeling of shared significance and reason inside the relationship, adjusting individual qualities and desires to make a bound-together vision for what's in store.

6. Positive Connections and Joy: Imbue delight, perkiness, and inspiration into everyday associations. Focus on shared encounters, giggling, and immediacy, encouraging an environment of affection, bliss, and good cheer inside the relationship.

7. Embracing Change and Growth: Embrace change and look for new encounters together. Move toward difficulties as any open doors for development and reestablishment, adjusting to life's changes with versatility, adaptability, and a development outlook.

8. Gratitude and Appreciation: Practise appreciation and appreciation for one another's presence, commitments, and characteristics. Develop a culture of appreciation and affirmation, praising each other's assets and endeavours.

9. Conflict Goal and Compromise: Move toward clashes with compassion, regard, and a readiness to think twice about. Look for goals through helpful exchange, understanding, and a pledge to track down commonly gainful arrangements.

10. Renewal and Reflection: Consistently think about the excursion of your relationship, commending achievements, accomplishments, and snapshots of development. Embrace reestablishment as a ceaseless course of recommitment and rediscovery, sustaining the connection between accomplices over the long haul.

By coordinating these bits of knowledge and practices into your marriage, you can develop a prospering organisation grounded in affection, understanding, and common help. Embrace the extraordinary force of positive brain science standards to make a marriage that blossoms with association, versatility, and shared satisfaction.

Encouraging couples to embark on a journey of ongoing growth, connection, and mutual support

Empowering couples to set out on an excursion of continuous development, association, and shared help is an extraordinary greeting that cultivates strength, closeness, and satisfaction inside the relationship. This is the way to rouse couples to embrace this excursion:

1. Embrace the Idea of Long lasting Learning: Urge couples to see their relationship as an excursion of consistent development and revelation. Stress the significance of gaining from encounters, embracing difficulties, and developing together over the long haul.

2. Promote Open Communication: Stress the meaning of transparent correspondence as the underpinning of areas of strength for an associated organisation. Urge couples to make a place of refuge for sharing contemplations, sentiments, and desires unafraid of judgement or analysis.

3. Celebrate Shared Values and Goals: Help couples recognize and commend their common qualities, objectives, and desires. Urge them to adjust their singular desires to an aggregate vision for the future, encouraging a feeling of solidarity and reason inside the relationship.

4. Prioritise Quality Time Together: Feature the significance of focusing on quality time for association and closeness. Urge couples to cut out devoted time for significant discussions, shared exercises, and encounters that reinforce their bond.

5. Support Each Other's Growth: Cultivate a culture of help and support inside the relationship. Urge couples to advocate for each other's self-improvement, desires, and dreams, commending achievements and achievements en route.

6. Embrace Weakness and Empathy: Urge couples to embrace weakness and sympathy as fundamental parts of closeness and association. Assist them with perceiving the force of weakness in extending trust and cultivating profound closeness.

7. Cultivate a Feeling of Adventure: Motivate couples to embrace a feeling of experience and investigation inside their relationship. Urge them to search out new encounters, make enduring recollections, and challenge themselves to step outside their usual ranges of familiarity together.

8. Navigate Difficulties with Resilience: Recognize that each relationship faces difficulties and mishaps. Urge couples to move toward difficulties with versatility, persistence, and a pledge to manage challenges together.

9. Practice Appreciation and Appreciation: Feature the significance of offering thanks and appreciation for one another's presence, endeavours, and commitments to the relationship. Urge couples to develop a culture of appreciation and affirmation in their day-to-day communications.

10. Celebrate Achievements and Ponder the Journey: Urge couples to commend achievements, commemorations, and snapshots of development together. Assist them with making ceremonies of reflection and festivity that honour the excursion they've shared and reaffirm their obligation to one another.

By empowering couples to leave on an excursion of continuous development, association, and common help, you enable them to develop a relationship that flourishes with affection, versatility, and shared satisfaction. Welcome them to embrace the experience of marriage with open hearts and a common obligation to sustain their bond for a long period of satisfaction and association.